TRAVEL SMARTS

TRAVEL SMARTS

EVERYTHING YOU NEED TO KNOW TO GO ANYWHERE

Second Edition

by Herbert Teison
and Nancy Dunnan

A Voyager Book

The
Globe
Pequot
press

Old Saybrook, Connecticut

The information in this book was confirmed at press time. The book's purpose is to provide accurate and authoritative information on the topics covered. It is sold with the understanding that neither the authors nor the publisher is rendering legal, financial, or other professional services. Neither the Globe Pequot Press nor the authors assume any liability resulting from action taken based on the information included herein. Mention of a company name does not constitute endorsement.

Library of Congress Cataloging-in-Publication Data

Teison, Herbert.
    Travel smarts: everything you need to know to go anywhere/by Herbert Teison and Nancy Dunnan. --2nd ed.
    p.   cm.
    "A Voyager book."
    Includes bibliographical references and index.
    ISBN 0-7627-0141-2
    1. Travel. I. Dunnan, Nancy. II. Title.
    G151.T44 1997
    910'.2'02--dc21
                                                            97-26256
                                                            CIP

This publication is a condensation from *Travel Smarts*, second edition, ©1995, 1997 by Herbert Teison and Nancy Dunnan, published by the Globe Pequot Press, Inc.

Manufactured in the United States of America
Second Edition/Third Printing

CONTENTS

INTRODUCTION

T RAVEL, whether to the next town or the next continent, can be a great joy. It introduces you to new and unusual places, to different peoples, cultures, and lifestyles. It is also a wonderful way to renew one's spirit, to spend time with family and friends, to learn a new activity or language—even to appreciate home. Yet the joy of travel can be ruined or at least diminished if you're not properly informed and adequately protected, if you pick the wrong place, become ill, spend too much money, or get "taken."

That's what *Travel Smarts* is all about: information and protection. As the publisher and managing editor of the *Travel Smart Newsletter,* we are devoted to telling you how to travel better for less, how to protect yourself against the unpleasant and often expensive mistakes one can make when leaving home.

One of the most important messages we can give you is that travel products—airline tickets, hotel rooms, rental-car reservations, etc.—are like unrefrigerated food; they're perishable. In days gone by, before supermarkets had huge refrigeration compartments and before they were open on Sundays, grocery store owners would reduce the prices of their fruits and vegetables on Saturday night before they closed. They knew that by Monday their unsold produce, if spoiled, would be worth nothing. This is how it is in the travel business, too. The unsold plane seat, the empty cruise cabin or hotel room, the unfilled space on a tour, the rental car sitting on the lot all bring in zero revenue, and the airline, cruise line, hotel owner, or tour operator loses money if you're not on board.

Even cities, states, and countries worry when tourism is down. Tourism income from one year can't be recovered the next; you can't store tourism and sell it later. No matter that visits to Chicago were up 3 percent in the past year; if they're down this year, the travel business in the Windy City suffers a loss that can never be recouped.

Because these travel suppliers know their wares are perishable, they do everything possible to sell as much of their capacity as they can, right now. To do so, to get you to book, they offer a variety of incentives, including better prices, free amenities, upgrades, and all kinds of extras.

Understandably, these suppliers don't want their other customers (the one who paid full price) to know that you're getting a better deal. One way they accomplish this is by giving you a discount without calling it one, by using euphemistic terms like "early bird special," "corporate rate," "two-for-one," "frequent-flyer bonus," and "senior citizen special."

Of course, there's much more to traveling smart than getting a good price. When you describe your trip to friends or look at your favorite snapshot, probably the last thing that comes to mind is what you paid for the experience. In fact, a year later, unless it was a truly great bargain, you may not even remember the price. It's unlikely that you'll be saying "Boy, we went to London, Paris, and Rome, and it only cost us $116.37 a day." What you will remember are the experiences, the people, the food, the scenery, the glorious hotel room or fabulous resort.

Although airlines, hotels, and car rental companies at times give the store away, most of the time you must be a good shopper and know where to look, how to speak up, and what the fine print means. To help you, in the following pages we examine each category of travel supplier, telling you about our favorites and giving you hundreds of insider tips that you can put to immediate use.

This book, like our newsletter, *Travel Smart*, will tell you how to travel better for less. We hope that being armed with all this good insider information will help make your next journey and the ones that follow full of joy.

1

MONEY MATTERS

If you will be a traveler, have always . . . two bags very full, that is, one of patience and another of money.

— John Florio

JOHN FLORIO was right. A key to enjoyable travel is to have enough money and to be careful spending it. You don't need to be paranoid, however, or you may miss all the fun. But ignoring the money issue or spending too much will certainly spoil a good time.

The first step, before going anywhere but around the block, is to figure out the real cost of your trip, whether it's for business or pleasure. If it's for business, your company will determine how much you can spend—whether you fly first class or coach, stay in a luxury suite or a budget hotel. But if you're the one calling the shots, it's tempting to ignore the economics involved until you get home and your credit-card charges start rolling in. So next time, before taking off, get a general idea of your costs by filling in the Vacation/Travel Budget worksheet that follows. You may not change a thing, but at least you'll know whether you're spending several hundred dollars or several thousand. Note the ubiquitous category "other." We've put that in because many travelers dash out to the mall and load up on new clothes, luggage, toiletries, even cameras, just for one trip, often without thinking about it. These purchases become part of a travel budget and, if you're not careful, can run up the total tab. Of course you may indeed need a new bathing suit or a black-tie jacket for a formal cruise, or the kids may require something beyond tattered jeans and sneakers for their trip to visit grandparents. Just keep track.

To control spending fill out the worksheet on the next page before purchasing tickets or making a deposit on a tour.

BEFORE LEAVING HOME

You also want to protect the things you leave behind you—your house or apartment and the valuables inside. Just as you do, robbers, love it when you go on vacation, and an empty house is an inviting target. For a trouble-free trip, follow these twelve tips:

1. *Leave a low-wattage light burning* inside your house and attach timers to several other lights, arranging for them to turn on and off at different times in different areas.
2. *Turn on a radio,* preferably tuned to a talk station.
3. *Arrange for someone to cut your grass,* rake the leaves, and raise and lower your blinds and curtains at random.
4. *Ask the post office* to hold your mail, and put a temporary stop on newspaper delivery. Alternatively, have someone pick up your mail or papers every day.
5. *Have a friend or neighbor house-sit,* or hire someone to check your house regularly. Pipes can freeze, roofs can leak, and furnaces can go on the blink.
6. *Give your itinerary,* with dates and telephone numbers, plus your auto license number and an extra house key, to someone reliable.
7. *Prepare a written record* of your credit-card numbers and the telephone numbers of the credit-card companies; keep them in a separate place from the credit cards themselves.

Vacation/Travel Budget

TOTAL AMOUNT I CAN AFFORD $_____

Packaged tour costs $_____

Airline, train, bus tickets $_____

Bus/taxi to airport/train station $_____

Car rental $_____

My car costs (gas, oil, tolls) $_____

Lodging cost (per night: $_____)   Total: $_____

Food (per day: $_____)   Total: $_____

Tickets to theater, museums, sites $_____

Fees (parking, campsites, etc.) $_____

Telephone calls to home/office $_____

Souvenirs and gifts $_____

Vaccinations/medical supplies $_____

Equipment rental/purchase $_____

Tips and taxes $_____

Kids' allowance $_____

Other $_____

Step 1: Determine the total amount you can spend.

Step 2: If you're taking a tour, find out if the price includes meals, all transportation, tips, and taxes, as well as admission fees.

Step 3: Enter dollar amounts into the appropriate categories.

Step 4: If you're over your budget, reduce spending for gifts or souvenirs, get a friend to drive you to and from the airport, and/or cut the length of your vacation.

8. *Arrange in advance for pet care,* as kennels are often booked solid during peak travel seasons.
9. *Have your car thoroughly serviced* prior to your trip and check the condition of your spare tire.
10. *Pack a roadside emergency kit* containing a flashlight, flares, and jumper cables.
11. *Assemble a first-aid kit* and include items for sunburn, bug bites, motion sickness, and diarrhea.
12. *Check the locks on all house windows and doors* before leaving; don't forget the door between the garage and your house.

Finally, don't hide the key under a doormat, in a flowerpot, or on a window ledge. Professional thieves know to look in all these places.

GETTING YOUR PASSPORT

If you don't have a passport or if you need to renew yours, here's the red tape involved and how to cut through some of it. Applications are available at 2,500 courthouses, 900 post offices, and 13 passport agencies in major cities. It can take a month or even six weeks to get a passport, depending on demand.

The State Department has a new service that will provide up-to-the-minute details on applying for a new passport or renewing an old one. Call National Passport Information Center, (900) 225-5674. You'll be charged 35 cents per minute.

To obtain your first passport, you must apply in person and provide:

- Proof of U.S. citizenship and a Social Security number
- Two identical 2x2-inch photos taken within the last six months; must be of your head against a plain background
- Proof of identity, such as a driver's license or birth certificate
- The fee

Note: To prove U.S. citizenship, bring a certified copy of your birth certificate if you were born in the United States. If you were born abroad you can use your certificate of naturalization or certificate of citizenship. If you can't get any of these items, call the nearest U.S. Passport Agency for assistance.

To renew a passport you must do so within twelve years of the date of issue. Passports are issued for ten years, but you get a two-year grace period. You can apply by mail, even if your passport has expired. Submit application, your old passport, two identical photos, and your check or money order (made out to Passport Services) to: National Passport Center, Box 371971, Pittsburgh, PA 15250.

The U.S. State Department recommends making a photocopy of the page in your passport with your passport number and biographical data. Take it with you and keep it in a safe place separate from your passport. If your passport is lost, a U.S. embassy or consulate can use this photocopy to expedite replacement of your passport. (The photocopy does not need to be notarized.)

CAUTION ☞ Many countries require that your passport be valid for six months *after* your intended return. If it's not, you may not be able to take your trip.

If You're in a Hurry

A company called Travisa works with travel agents and the public to get both passports and visas issued quickly, sometimes even in the same day. Its headquarters are in Washington, D.C., with branches in Chicago, Detroit, San Francisco, and Puerto Rico. Call (800) 222-2589.

Or you can pay an extra $30 to the National Passport Information Center's "Expedite Service" and get a passport in three business days—that's three business days after they receive all the necessary papers. Call (900) 225-5674.

Faster service is also available if you can show plane tickets or confirmed reservations proving you're traveling abroad within ten days.

INSURING YOUR TRIP

Four things are guaranteed to spoil a trip and cost you money: (1) not being able to go due to illness or some other emergency, (2) having the packager or tour operator cancel the trip, (3) losing your luggage, or (4) getting sick while away from home. Various types of travel insurance can provide some degree of protection against such unhappinesses and reduce your potential expenses. Before leaving home, take time to figure out if you need to buy extra protection. Here are the three types of travel insurance you need to know about.

1. *Trip-cancellation coverage:* Many insurance agents, cruise lines, and insurance companies sell this type of coverage, with prices that range widely. (**TIP** Never buy insurance sold by the operator/packager. If the company declares bankruptcy, the coverage won't be valid.) Two independent companies that have reasonably priced policies are Travel Guard International, underwritten by CNA Insurance Company and sold by ASTA Marketing Services of Stevens Point, Wisconsin (715-345-0505), and Access America, underwritten by BCS Insurance Company and sold by Access America Service Corp. of Richmond, Virginia (804-285-3300). Call for current rates.
2. *Personal-property coverage:* Check your homeowners policy regarding personal-property coverage worldwide. It may protect you against lost or delayed luggage, or if you have a special floater for your camera, jewelry, and other valuables, you may not need additional insurance.

$ TIP Airlines accept liability for up to $1,250 per passenger for bags lost or damaged between points within the United States, and up to $9.07 a pound for checked bags and $400 per passenger for unchecked bags on most but not all international flights; however, the airlines cover only the depreciated value of lost possessions, not the replacement cost.
$ TIP Report any luggage problem before you leave the airport and insist that a missing-luggage report be filled out, even if the airline officials tell you it will be on the next flight;

it may not. Specify that your luggage is to be delivered to your hotel or home free of charge.

3. *Medical coverage:* See pages 207–10 for a complete discussion of this important topic

TAKING ALONG MONEY

Once you know about how much your trip will cost, you'll need to decide what form of money to take along. We think it's smart to carry a mixture—cash, checks, traveler's checks, and credit cards—because each one has advantages in certain situations. When abroad, for instance, plan to use credit cards for major purchases such as rental cars, hotels, and restaurants, yet have enough foreign currency with you to cover the first day's expenses: transportation from the airport or train station to your hotel, tips, and immediate needs. Then convert traveler's checks to cash on an as-you-need-it basis. Banks almost always give you better exchange rates than do hotels, stores, or private exchange booths.

Two things there's no debate about: Carry small bills and change, and never flash large bills. To do so is asking for trouble.

Cash

You'll obviously need enough pocket money to pay for the taxi or bus from the airport or train station to your hotel or, if you're driving, for tolls and incidentals. **CAUTION** Wearing a fanny pack or money belt around your waist advertises both your status as a tourist and precisely where you've put your cash or credit cards.

$ TIP Fool thieves by keeping only incidentals in these packs or bags (notebook, map, pencil, sunglasses, stamps, mints, Handiwipes, etc.) and hide your money and passport in an underarm or shoulder belt or pack, or around your waist and under your clothing.

Traveler's Checks

Traveler's checks are issued by American Express, First National City Bank, Thomas Cook and Sons, and other companies. If you use American Express, you'll also be able to have your mail held at American Express offices around the world.

More than half the American Express traveler's checks are sold without fees through various travel groups, such as the American Automobile Association, or at local banks. Senior citizens often get them for free at their bank, so shop around and ask.

Traveler's checks are sold in a variety of denominations. Make two copies of the list of numbers on your checks before leaving home. Leave one copy with a friend or your lawyer or accountant and carry one with you, keeping it in a separate place from the checks themselves. You should also keep separate the written directions for replacing lost or stolen checks that accompanied the new checks you purchased. If you're traveling with someone else, divide the checks between you, so if one of you loses them or is robbed you'll still have some left.

Although traveler's checks are safe and replaceable if lost or stolen, you do pay a fee to purchase them and often a service charge when cashing them.

Converting checks (or changing money) at hotels can cost 3 to 4 percent over the usual exchange rate in a foreign country. The best place to cash checks is the issuer's service office or a bank. Avoid airport money changers; they usually have the worst exchange rates and highest fees.

$ TIP Thomas Cook does not charge a commission if you cash its checks at any of its U.S. or foreign outlets.

Also avoid using traveler's checks to pay for meals in foreign countries without getting details first. Many overseas restaurants have exchange rates that penalize you 5 to 10 percent. For example, Fofi's Estiatorio, a chic Berlin eatery, doesn't take credit cards and charges 15 marks (about $10) to cash a $100 traveler's check. If you have difficulty with the language, ask the hotel concierge to call the restaurant and ask about its policy.

Be smart and purchase some traveler's checks in foreign currencies to escape currency fluctuations and poor exchange rates; this way you'll avoid a fee when cashing them in that country. American Express, Thomas Cook, VISA, and MasterCard sell traveler's checks denominated in leading currencies, such as the

British pound, the German mark, and the French franc. This enables you also to lock in exchange rates before leaving the United States.

$ TIP To buy foreign-currency traveler's checks without having to leave home, contact Ruesch International at (800) 424–2923 or (800) 292–4685.

Don't go overboard, however, with foreign denomination checks; those that you don't cash will have to be converted back into dollars, running up a needless exchange fee.

Automatic Teller Machine Cards

ATM cards reduce the need to carry a lot of cash, whether you're traveling near home or abroad. CIRRUS and PLUS now have ATMs in many foreign countries, but they are not identical to their U.S. counterparts. You should know the following:

- ATMs outside North America generally do not accept personal identification numbers (PINs) longer than four digits. Check with your bank to see if you need a PIN that machines abroad will accept.
- The keypads on many foreign ATMs do not include letters, so learn the corresponding numerals by checking a telephone keypad.
- Not all foreign ATMs are open twenty-four hours a day.
- ATMs automatically take funds from your account, and daily withdrawal limits do apply, so transfer enough money into your account before leaving the country.
- When you use an ATM bank card abroad; you get the "wholesale" rate, the rate that normally applies to transactions of $1 million or more. This rate is often 5 percent better than the rate tourists get when they cash traveler's checks in a hotel, but ATM transactions usually have a flat fee, from 90 cents to $1.50.

If you're getting $500 of foreign currency, you'll get as much as $25 more by using an ATM machine outside a foreign bank or American Express office than by cashing traveler's checks at their teller windows inside.

Credit Cards

Another way to travel without carrying large amounts of cash is to take a credit card. When you use a credit card in a foreign country, the rate of exchange that applies is not the prevailing one at the time that you make a purchase or pay for your hotel room or rental car; rather, it is the rate that prevails when the transaction is processed by the credit-card company. The rate could, therefore, be higher or lower than the one at the time you actually use the card. Keep these two points in mind:

- When making a large purchase, use your credit card *if* it carries buyer protection. You will then have some recourse if the product is faulty.
- Credit cards are also best for purchasing packaged tours; airline, bus, and railroad tickets; and car rentals because these vendors may take as much as 8 percent if you use traveler's checks. And if you have a problem with a tour operator or airline that goes out of business, you will have some recourse.

Most hotels will ask you for an imprint of your credit card when you check in. Some, often without telling you, will arbitrarily block (limit) up to $2,000 in charges because they want to make sure they get paid first should you go over your spending limit while on your vacation or trip. To avoid this you can do one of two things: Ask the hotel clerk not to block charges against your credit limit or give them your Diners Club or American Express card, which does not have limits.

Here are two more ways to use your credit card to get better travel deals:

- If you use MCI or another long-distance telephone service, arrange to have your MCI bills paid by your credit card to get additional miles in an airline frequent-flyer mileage program.
- If you return home from abroad with more than the $400 duty-free allowance on goods, U.S. Customs will let you pay for your extra duty charges with a credit card.

PROTECTING YOUR MONEY

Purse-snatching and wallet-swiping can happen to anyone almost anywhere and anytime—at a restaurant, waiting for a train, in line for tickets, etc. You can foil thieves by taking a few preventive measures.

- *Carry only the credit cards you plan to use that day.* It's also a good idea to carry cash, credit cards, driver's license, and keys in separate locations—your purse, wallet, pockets, or briefcase. Then if someone grabs your wallet, for instance, he or she won't get all your valuables.
- *Carry just one or two checks,* not your full checkbook. Replenish as you use them.
- *Memorize the PIN for your bank card.* Don't write it down anywhere, and certainly not in your address book or checkbook.
- *Don't attach your address or telephone number* to your key chain.
- *Keep two up-to-date lists* (one at home, one at the office) of your credit-card account numbers, accompanied by their emergency telephone numbers.

If You Are Ripped Off

If your credit cards are stolen, immediately call to cancel them. And remember, you must write to the credit-card company within sixty days of receiving your bill in order to avoid being charged for items over $50 charged by thieves.

Report the theft to the police, keeping a copy of the report. You'll need this information to file an insurance claim or deduct losses on your federal income tax return.

Call your card company as soon as you discover trouble. Photocopy the list of credit-card emergency phone numbers below and carry it with you. (Call collect from abroad.)

- **AMERICAN EXPRESS**
  United States and Canada   (800) 635–5955
  Other countries   (910) 333–3211
  Optima   (910) 333–3211
- **DISCOVER**
  United States   (800) DISCOVER

Other countries	(801) 568-0205
• MASTERCARD	
United States	(800) 826-2181
Other countries	(314) 275-6690
• VISA	
United States	(800) VISA-911
Other countries	(415) 574-7700

If you lose your checkbook, immediately close your entire account; however, if only one or two checks were stolen, simply arrange for a stop payment on them.

If your ATM card is stolen, ask the bank to issue a new one, even if you didn't write the code number on anything taken by the thieves. Thieves know that many people use their birthday, wedding anniversary, or number sequences (2, 3, 4, 5, 6) for their codes. You will be held liable for $50 of fraudulent use of your ATM card if you report the loss within two days, but as much as $500 if you report it after two days.

To replace long-distance telephone credit cards, call their toll-free numbers:

AT&T	(800) 225-5200
Sprint	(800) 877-4646
MCI	(800) 444-4444

Safeguarding Your Purchases

Items purchased while traveling and paid for by credit card may be protected. The best way to find out is to call your credit-card issuer before you begin your travels. Issuer coverage seems to change almost every month. Some guidelines:

- *STANDARD CARDS.* Citibank, AT&T, Universal, Chemical, and American Express have purchase protection. Best deal: AmEx, which covers up to $1,000 per incident. Citibank has a limit of $250 per claim.
- *GOLD CARDS.* AmEx has a maximum of $50,000 over the life of the account and includes cameras and video equipment in checked baggage. AmEx's per-claim limit is $1,000.

GETTING YOUR MONEY BACK: VAT REFUNDS

While traveling in Europe, you'll encounter something called VAT, or Value-Added Tax, an indirect sales tax. (Canada has Goods and Services Tax [GST], which is similar to VAT.) VAT is charged or added to the cost of most purchases, hotel rooms, meals, train travel, and rental cars. Most countries allow a refund of the tax to foreigners. (Goods and services used in the country where you buy them, such as hotel rooms and car rentals, are not VAT refundable. Purchases taken out of the country, such as clothing, jewelry, and cosmetics, are fully or partially refundable.) It's worth taking the time to get the refund. VATs can be as much as 20 percent of your purchases, 28 percent in France on luxury items. The refund turns a pricey item into a bargain, almost.

There are four ways to get refunds:

- *Mail Refunds.* To obtain a refund by mail, make your purchase and pay the amount on the price tag, which includes the VAT. If you show your passport, however, the merchant will fill in (or have you fill in) tax-refund forms and will give you a copy of them, frequently with a self-addressed envelope. Some large department stores, such as Harrods in London and Galeries Lafayette in Paris, have offices to help with the paperwork.

  When you leave the country, your form is stamped by a customs official at the airport or frontier as proof of your departure from the country. You then mail the form back to the store. The store will send you a refund, typically in several weeks. In some cases if you paid with a credit card, your refund may be credited to your account. **TIP** Items purchased must be available for inspection by customs officials at the point of departure, so don't pack them at the bottom of your bag.

  If you purchased items with a credit card, ask the merchant or shopkeeper to put the purchase price on a charge form and put the VAT charges on a separate form. Ask that they hold the VAT charge until they have received official notification that you've left the country; then they tear up the VAT form.

- *Exit Refunds.* To get an exit refund, go through the same form-filling-out procedure, but when you leave the country, give the papers to a customs person and you'll get cash or a check on the spot. If it's a check, it will be in the local currency, and you can cash it at a bank at the airport and exchange it for dollars (or the currency of the next country on your itinerary).
- *Direct Export.* Some countries allow you to subtract the VAT from the purchase price if you pay the shopkeeper to mail your purchase to you at your U.S. address. **CAUTION** Shipping can be expensive, and you may have to pay U.S. import duty.
- *Europe Tax-Free Shopping (ETS).* This tax-refund specialist (Europe's largest) operates in about fifteen countries and has signed on about 60,000 individual merchants. Participants display a blue-and-red "Tax Free for Tourists" sticker in English. When you make a purchase at one of these shops, the merchant actually seals your purchase and issues a VAT refund check right on the spot.

  ETS has desks at the major airports and terminals, so you can cash your refund check in one of several currencies. If you happen to leave the country from an airport or border crossing where there is no ETS desk, you simply mail the check for a refund. On charge-card purchases, the ETS official can arrange to have the refund credited to your account.

Each country has its own regulations, which are subject to change at any time. As of now, only Austria, Canada, and Israel give refunds on lodging, meals, and car rentals. Most countries have brochures that explain their VAT rates and refunds.

When you receive your VAT refund check, it will probably be in the currency of the country where it was issued. Check with several U.S. banks, as service fees for cashing these checks vary widely, or use a foreign-exchange dealer. **BEST BET** Ruesch International, which charges $3.00 a check for walk-in or mail transactions. Ruesch has offices in New York, Washington, Chicago, Los Angeles, and Boston. You can also call (800) 292-4685.

Buy expensive items at stores participating in a tax-refund program, such as ETS. Try to make all your purchases in one large store where employees can do the paperwork. Use your credit card to get a better exchange rate on your purchase and your refund. Before leaving home, get a free brochure explaining VAT from ETS, (312) 382-1001 or (203) 965-5145.

SENDING MONEY IN A FLASH

If you need to send money to someone in the United States or abroad or if you're caught short, here are your choices:

• *FEDERAL GOVERNMENT.* The State Department operates a Citizens Emergency Funds Transfer Program for Americans who are stranded in a foreign country. Friends or relatives send the money to the State Department by credit-card charge through Western Union, in the form of a cashier's check or money order, or by overnight mail or bank wire transfer. Personal checks are not accepted. The citizen overseas receives the money in local currency. *How fast:* Usually the same day or the next day. *How much:* Same as Western Union's international service plus a $15 consulate fee. *How to do it:* Call the State Department at (202) 647-5225.

• *BANKS.* You can have money wired from your bank account at home to a foreign bank, provided your home bank has a branch office in the country you're visiting. You should set up this procedure before leaving home. *How fast:* Same day, domestically; next business day, internationally. *How much:* Fee varies; average is $25 to $45. *How to do it:* Call your local bank.

• *U.S. POSTAL SERVICE.* The Postal Service will not send cash through the mail. However, you can send a money order if it's going domestically; for international destinations use a bank draft (a check) in the currency of the country to which it's going. Bank drafts are available from most foreign-exchange brokers, such as Ruesch International, Thomas Cook, Citibank, or American Express. *How fast:* Express Mail has next-day delivery

GET BACK YOUR VAT

Use a service. Popular with business travelers, this company will cut through the red tape and do all the work for you. There's no up-front charge, but there is a fee, contingent upon the amount of your VAT rebate. For information contact Meridian VAT Reclaim, 578 Eighth Avenue, New York, NY 10018; (212) 554-6600.

Minimum Purchase Required for VAT Refund Eligibility

In many countries you need to make a minimum purchase at a particular store to be eligible for a VAT refund. You might want to make as many purchases as possible at one store. Ask before shopping.

Country	VAT	Minimum Purchase per Store
Austria	20.0%	1001 schillings (about $90)
Belgium	19.5%	5,000 francs (about $150)
Britain	17.5%	None, although some stores require £25–£50 (about $35–$80)
Denmark	20.0%	600 kroner (about $93)
France	18.6%	1,200 francs (about $250)
Germany	5.0%	None, but stores may set minimum
Italy	19.0%	300,000 lire (about $200)
Netherlands	17.5%	350 guilders (about $185)
Spain	6.0%	10,000 pesetas (about $95)
Switzerland	6.5%	500 francs/item (about $340)

within the United States and to most foreign countries. *How much:* Up to eight ounces, domestically, $10.75; internationally, $15 to $20, depending on the country. There's a $4.50 pickup fee; no fee if you take it to the post office. *How to do it:* Call your local post office, or call (800) 222-1811.

• *AMERICAN EXPRESS.* Money can be transferred from American Express service centers or agents through its "MoneyGram" service. *How fast:* About ten minutes to most places. *How much:* Fees vary, depending on the amount being sent and destination. Up to $100 costs $13; up to $500 is $39, and up to $10,000 is $399. *How to do it:* MoneyGrams are sold at travel-agency offices, American Express travel offices, airports, auto clubs, grocery and convenience stores, packaging/postal outlets, and check cashers. You can pay for the transfer with cash, Visa, MasterCard, or Discover as well as with American Express. Outside the United States, however, you must pay with cash. Call (800) 926-9400 for nearest location and taped information.

• *WESTERN UNION.* Western Union has a similar plan and accepts MasterCard, Discover, and Visa for telephone transfers. If you prefer, you can go in person to any one of many Western Union agencies and pay by cash or certified check. *How fast:* Immediately if paid for with cash; fifteen minutes if using a credit card. *How much:* Fees vary according to amount and destination: $100 sent domestically is $15 if paid for with cash and $25 if with a credit card; internationally, fee varies. *How to do it:* Call (800) 325-4176.

Travel Smart Newsletter has an attractive, thin, easy-to-read slide rule that converts foreign currency, weights, and measurements. Send $5.00 to Travel Smart, 40 Beechdale Road, Dobbs Ferry, NY 10522.

MAKING TELEPHONE CALLS

Long-Distance Calls from the United States

If you don't have enough change to make a long-distance call from a pay phone, or if you don't want the call to be charged to the phone you're using, you can, of course, call collect. Most of us dial 0 + the area code + the number. But you can save up to 44 percent if you dial (800) COLLECT, using MCI. You can call anywhere in the United States and to more than one hundred foreign countries this way; however, the calls must be made from the United States or Puerto Rico. Another alternative: Dial (800) OPERATOR and use AT&T's plan, which is similar. You can also ask how much the call will cost ahead of time.

Long-Distance Dialing within the United States

With the relatively new American Travel Network (ATN) Discount Calling Card, the cost anywhere in the United States, including Hawaii, Alaska, Puerto Rico, and the U.S. Virgin Islands, day or night, is just 17.5 cents per minute. The card is free, and there's no monthly fee or monthly minimum-usage requirements. See the table on page 19 for cost comparisons between ATN calls and those made through other companies.

$ TIP Avoid making credit-card calls from pay phones unless you know how much they'll cost. Privately owned pay phones have sprung up around the country, and although they must charge the going local rate for coin calls, they can charge whatever they wish for credit-card calls. BEST BET Pay cash for local calls and ask the operator for the price of long-distance calls made with a credit card.

Long-Distance Calls from Abroad

Getting the right local currency for calls or dealing with a foreign operator who speaks only the local language make long-distance calls in foreign countries somewhat intimidating. One way around this problem: USA Direct Service. By dialing a special access code, you're automatically connected to an English-speaking operator. Calls are billed to your AT&T Calling Card, AT&T Universal Card, or a local telephone company card, or they can be placed collect. The service is available in more than 120 countries. It also makes it possible to get 800 numbers in the United States, including those for travel agents, airlines, and hotels, as well as directory assistance for other numbers. For information call USA Direct Service and World Connect Service at (800) 331–1140 or (412) 553–7458.

Calling Home

Use your credit card when making long-distance calls from a hotel or motel room. Direct-dial calls are assessed at about 40 percent. You can access your particular long-distance carrier by dialing the correct number:

AT&T	(800) 3210–ATT or (800) 225–5288
MCI	(800) 674–7000
Sprint	(800) 877–4646

When making several credit-card calls from your hotel or motel room, don't hang up in between calls; instead, press the pound (#) key to get a new dial tone and to avoid a fee from the hotel for each separate call.

Three-Minute Daytime Call from New York City to Los Angeles

	Surcharge	Cost/Minute	Total
ATN Card	$0.00	$0.175	$0.53
AT&T	.85	.37	1.96
MCI	.83	.37	1.94
Sprint	.85	.37	1.96

Note: ATN is a division of Hospitality Services Group, which has more than 15,000 members, including pilots and business travelers; for information call (800) 477–9692.

Prepaid Telephone Cards

These are often a very good deal for travelers—they're easy to use, available everywhere (convenience stores, gas stations, post offices), and often cheaper for short, long-distance calls than other services. For instance, a card purchased in London provides cheaper U.K. to U.S. rates than one purchased at home.

But don't buy just any prepaid card . . . there are plenty of fly-by-night operators in this business. Stick with known names, such as AT&T, MCI, Sprint, Western Union, PTT Telekom, and FirstClass (sold at U.S. post offices). Follow these protective steps:

1. Know what you're paying for. For international calls, find out how many units it takes to make a one-minute call.
2. Don't accept a card that charges access fees each time you use it.
3. Make sure it has an 800 customer service number (on the back of the card or listed below).
4. If you're on the road a lot, buy only a card that is rechargeable. Otherwise, make sure it won't expire before you get back home.
5. If you have any questions or problems, contact the International Telecard Association, (800) 333-3513.

$ TIP Sprint's Spree prepaid card has a great advantage when it comes to calling in foreign countries: It automatically lets you know how much value is left—not in foreign currency but in minutes of talk time.

CAUTION There are more than 500 companies selling prepaid phone cards; many go out of business every day. That means picking the wrong card can spell disaster. In response to the growing problems and complaints, the following three organizations have put together a useful brochure with important tips for purchasing a card. To get a copy contact one of these sources:

- Better Business Bureau, 257 Park Avenue South, New York, NY 10010
- Federal Trade Commission, Public Reference, Washington, DC 20580; (202) 362-2222

Customer Service Numbers for Prepaid Cards	
AT&T	(800) 462-1818
Amerivex	(800) 827-6299
FirstClass	(800) 297-2600
MCI	(800) 830-9444
PTT TeleKom	(800) 839-9916
Speedway	(800) 801-7740
Sprint	(800) 366-0707
UniTel	(800) 242-9856
WaWa	(800) 603-5085
Western Union	(800) 374-0909

• New York State Attorney General Dennis C. Vacco, The Capitol, Albany, NY 12224 (or 120 Broadway, New York, NY 10271); (800) 771-7755.

Weather Wake-up Call

Dial the Weather Channel's new service at 900-WEATHER and select option 6. Pick a time within a twenty-four-hour period and you'll be called at that exact time with the day's weather. Away from home? Dial 800-WEATHER from any touchtone phone and charge the wake-up call to a credit card. In both cases, there is a 95 cents per minute charge.

2

CHEAP AIR TRAVEL

The most dangerous aspect of flying is driving to the airport.

—Anonymous

Most travelers don't realize (or have never stopped to think about it) that the difference in cost to an airline between an occupied seat and an empty one is minimal. The pilots, ground crew, and cabin attendants get the same pay regardless of whether or not the seats are filled. Fuel cost is almost identical, and so is just about everything else with the exception of meals. If an airline has to feed you, then it must spend another $3.00 to $10.00 per passenger; meals served to first-class passengers cost the airlines slightly more, as do specially ordered meals, but both are included in the cost of your ticket.

Given that the cost to fly a plane from, say, Houston to Chicago is about the same whether it's filled or not, airlines knock themselves out to get the maximum number of people in seats on each flight. Each additional passenger is a profit center. This, of course, is a plus for you because it leads to fare wars, discounts, and seasonally reduced priced tickets.

If you've ever flown late in the afternoon or on a weekend, you'll notice that the plane is likely to be partially empty. On the other hand, early-morning flights and the last flights before the weekend are oversold on popular routes. Why? Business traffic. The airlines love business travelers: They are their bread and butter, paying top dollar for air fare, and they demand a full schedule. Business fliers know when they want to fly, and they want the planes to be available to take them.

Pleasure travelers are much more flexible, willing to fly on weekends or holidays and at slack times, *if* they can get a fair deal. They are what the airlines call "price sensitive." Most airlines look first to business travelers to fill their seats at standard (translate, "high") prices and then fill in the unsold seats with leisure travelers at whatever price gets them to go. It's all done through something called "capacity control."

Deep in the recesses of an airline's headquarters, an operator sits in front of a computer screen. The mission: Make Flight 000 at 9:27 A.M. from Atlanta to Dallas on Wednesday, November 24 (a year from now), as full (profitable) as possible. This is called "yield management," getting the most money for any given flight. Yield management basically consists of loading in the flight with business travelers (predicting when they will go) at top dollar, then filling the vacant seats with pleasure flyers, many at discount prices. The airlines differentiate between the two by putting restrictions on discount seats, such as advance purchase and weekend stayovers—restrictions that most business travelers will not hold still for. You can't beat the system; don't even try.

One thing you can beat: the domino effect. Take flights that leave early in the day. Takeoffs are so tightly scheduled that a single foul-up can lead to a chain of delays. So the earlier your flight, the more likely you won't be a victim of the domino effect.

The Best Time to Buy Airline Tickets

Don't buy tickets on weekends. Many airlines test fare increases by raising prices on Friday nights, Saturdays, and Sundays, when fewer tickets are sold; if other carriers don't follow suit, the prices come down on Monday.

Tax Deductions

A company can deduct the extra cost of extending an employee's business trip over a Saturday night to obtain a lower, excursion airfare. Food and lodging costs incurred during an extra day qualify as a business expense, even if no business is conducted on the extra day, provided that the airfare reduction reduces the overall cost of the trip (IRS Ruling).

SMART AIR-TRAVEL TIPS

Getting the best deal on your next flight takes more than simply calling your agent or the airlines. Here are sixteen ways you can get on board as inexpensively as possible.

1. *Plan in advance.* Tickets purchased fourteen, twenty-one, or forty-five days in advance are less expensive than tickets purchased closer to departure day.
2. *Choose the right airport.* Fares are actually higher at some airports than at others. The highest are at the so-called fortress hubs where just about all the flights are controlled by a single airline. Drive to a nearby airport where there's real competition to save money. For example, from Pittsburgh to Louisville round-trip was $274, but from Cleveland, a 2½-hour drive away, it was just $103 to Louisville. Or, make a stop. Flying from New York to St. Louis is at least $100 cheaper if you stop in Detroit. So get out your map and talk with your travel agent about alternative airports.
3. *Buy your ticket as early as possible* after reading about a discount rate in the newspaper. If at any time before you depart the airline announces a lower fare than what you paid, you may be entitled to buy at the lower rate. Ask your travel agent to handle this for you. When buying your ticket, book the best airline seat you can get. Then get to the airport fifty to sixty minutes before flight time and ask at the gate if a better seat is available. Most airlines save

some good seats (aisle, window, front cabin) for high-mileage frequent flyers and business travelers paying full fare. One hour before departure these seats are usually freed up.

4. *Pick an inexpensive time to fly.* Night fares (usually after 7:00 P.M. may be cheaper than daytime fares. Weekend fares can be lower on routes heavily used by business travelers during the week but not on weekends. Fares to vacation destinations such as Hawaii, Florida, the Caribbean, or ski slopes can be lower if you travel Monday through Thursday because most people want to leave on Friday, Saturday, or Sunday. Lastly, off-season fares tend to be lower than in high season. For example, it's cheaper to fly to Florida in August than in January.

5. *Use a travel agent.* Although a ticket purchased from an agent will cost the same as from an airline, a good agent, through continual computer monitoring, can instantly tell you which carrier has the best fare to your destination. (Agents get about the same commission from all airlines: approximately 10 percent domestic and 8–11 percent foreign.) As a rule travel agents do not sell for less than the fare prices listed in their computers. If you are a good customer, however, they may indeed give you a small discount, which comes out of their commission, or they may buy from consolidators (see page 30) and give you a larger discount.

Insider Tips

How to Get an Empty Seat Next to Yours: Request an aisle seat in the center of a wide-bodied plane. Agents typically book middle seats last. If you're traveling with someone else, book one aisle seat and one window seat in a three-seat row. If you're a frequent flyer or a business traveler, ask to be assigned to a "preferred" section where the middle seats are held to the last minute.

In addition ask your agent if he or she can help you with what we call "ploys," some of which are legal, others, borderline. For example:

- Back-to-back ticketing is a ploy whereby you avoid a required Saturday night stayover on cut-rate tickets by purchasing two or more sets and switching around the dates. **CAUTION ☛** Some airlines have declared this illegal.
- Hidden-city ticketing occurs when you purchase a ticket to a major city for a price lower than the one to the intermediate city where you actually want to deplane. You have only carry-on luggage because checking it will result in either losing the bags (because they'd be sent to the final destination) or blowing the deal. Airlines don't like this ploy but find it hard to prevent.

6. *Book early-in-the-day flights.* Then if the flight is canceled, you have more options for flying out the same day and avoid getting stuck overnight.
7. *Fly the upstarts.* There is a bus, the M103, that goes down the west side of Manhattan to Forty-second Street. Passengers on that bus don't expect a cabin attendant,

Basic, No-Frills Carriers

If all you want is transportation, you'll save money with these airlines:

America West	(800) 235-9292
Carnival	(800) 437-2110
Kiwi Air	(800) 538-5494
Midway	(800) 446-4392
Midwest Express	(800) 452-2022
Reno Air	(800) 736-6247
Southwest Airlines	(800) 435-9792
Sun Jet	(800) 478-6538
Tower Air	(800) 221-2500
ValuJet	(800) 825-8538

meals, or even a snack. All they want to do is get downtown. If you adopt this attitude when flying, you'll find it a whole lot less frustrating. Expect only transportation. Don't expect the ride to change your life.

8. *Convention fares.* If you are going to a convention, your organization may have made arrangements with one or more airlines for discounts. Check with the people running the show. If the airlines giving the discount do not fly from your local airport, it may pay to drive to one where they do.

9. *Bereavement fares.* If a close relative dies and you need to fly to the funeral, the airlines will give you a lower fare—15 to 50 percent off full price. Some (Continental and TWA as of press time) also offer reduced fares for those visiting an immediate member of the family who is critically ill. The requirements for bereavement fares vary widely from carrier to carrier, so check with your travel agent or directly with the airlines.

10. *Senior coupons.* The older crowd is a prime marketing target for all airlines; presumably, these people have all the time in the world and money to spend. One of the best deals the airlines offers is a coupon book, available to those who are sixty-two and older. Proof of age is required when you purchase the booklets and sometimes upon boarding. The coupons, purchased through your travel agent or directly from the airline, are sold in packets of four and eight coupons, with each coupon good for a one-way ticket from your originating city to your destination. Coupons are valid for domestic and, in some cases, Canadian flights but not for international flights. Coupon deals vary, but a typical one is United's "Silver Pack," which gives passengers over age sixty-two four tickets, good for travel anywhere in the continental United States.

    CAUTION ☛ Coupons expire one year from date of purchase, and reservations must be made two weeks in advance. Book early because only a certain number of seats are available on each flight for coupon holders.

$ TIP USAirways lets seniors use coupons for an accompanying child age two to eleven, whereas TWA sells a book of coupons for a companion of any age plus a 20 percent discount on a ticket to Europe. *Ask.*

11. *Senior discounts.* Most major airlines give 10 percent off rates for those over age sixty-two on excursion fares, so always mention your age to your agent or the airline. One advantage these discounts have over senior coupons is that you can travel with a companion and the companion also gets 10 percent off, regardless of his or her age. (The two of you must travel on the same flight.) There are other variations on the theme, which come and go. For example, as we go to press, Virgin Atlantic is giving travelers over age sixty a 20-percent discount. (For more on airline discounts for seniors, see p. 162.)

    $ TIP Ask about senior discounts for "off-peak" days (Tuesday, Wednesday, Thursday, and Saturday).

12. *The baby flies free.* Typically there is no charge for a child under age two sitting on the lap of an adult on domestic flights. Lately, however, for safety reasons, airlines have been encouraging passengers to purchase a separate seat for children, into which a child's seat will fit. Most offer baby fares at half price.

13. *Kids' fares.* When traveling with children, check out reduced fares. On American, for example, children traveling domestically in a seat of their own get between 50 and 65 percent off full fare. If the flight is going out of the country, the discount ranges from 10 to 75 percent off the full fare. Periodically airlines have "Kids-Go-Free" promotions—but only if the children are accompanied by a fare-paying adult.

HANDY REFERENCE: AIRLINE NUMBERS

Domestic

Alaska Airlines	(800) 426–0333
American Airlines	(800) 433–7300,
	(800) 237–7981
America West	(800) 235–9292
Continental Airlines	(800) 525–0280,
	(800) 441–1135
Delta Airlines	(800) 221–1212
Hawaiian Airlines	(800) 367–5320
Kiwi International	(800) 538–5494
Midwest Express	(800) 452–2022
Northwest Airlines	(800) 225–2525
Southwest Airlines	(800) 435–9792
TWA	(800) 221–2000
United Airlines	(800) 241–6522
USAirways	(800) 428–4322
Virgin Atlantic	(800) 862–8621

Foreign

Air Canada	(800) 776–3000
Aerolitoral	(800) 237–6639
Aeromexico	(800) 237–6639
Air France	(800) 237–2747
Alitalia	(800) 223–5730
British Airways	(800) 247–9297
British West Indies	(800) 327–7401
Canadian Airlines	(800) 426–7000
El Al	(800) 223–6700
Finnair	(800) 950–5000
Iberia	(800) 772–4642
KLM Royal Dutch	(800) 347–7747
Lufthansa	(800) 645–3880
Mexicana Airlines	(800) 531–7921
Sabena	(800) 950–1000
SAS	(800) 221–2350
Swissair	(800) 221–4750
TAP Air Portugal	(800) 221–7370

14. *Military fares.* Personnel on active duty, and often their dependents, get substantial discounts.
15. *Student fares.* These vary all over the place, depending on time of year, place, the student's age, and so on.
16. *Getting on a fully booked flight.* Move to the top of the waiting list by asking for a full-coach or first-class ticket. Discount ticketholders are typically at the bottom of the waiting list, whereas full-fare and standbys tend to get priority.

USING CONSOLIDATORS AND BUCKET SHOPS

About 20 percent of fliers go overseas on consolidator tickets, saving up to 50 percent off regular fares. This business—often called the "gray market" of ticket distribution—is probably the biggest secret of the airline industry. Consolidators are wholesalers who purchase airline tickets in bulk at huge discounts and then sell them at a discount to agents. These discounts range from 25 to 75 percent off retail airline tickets. Consolidators are able to land huge discounts because they buy in volume and they buy seats

Kids Alone in the Air

With the proliferation of non-nuclear families, kids are often sent alone to visit one of their parents in another city, or they may be going to visit other relatives. A flight attendant will seat the child in a special section of the plane, talk to him or her from time to time, provide games and special kids' meals, and deliver the child to the right people at the other end. Some airlines require that a child traveling alone be at least five years old for a through flight and eight years old for a connecting flight. Expect to pay a fee (around $30) if the child is on a connecting flight. **BEST BET** ✔ When booking an unaccompanied child on a connecting flight, select a flight that leaves early in the day. Avoid the last one because if the plane fails to take off, the child is left at night in an unfamiliar city.

Some Consolidators

C. L. Thompson	(415) 398-2535
Euro-Asia Express	(800) 782-9625
Hudson Holidays	(800) 323-6855
TFI Tours	(800) 745-8000,
	(212) 736-1140
Travac Tours	(800) 872-8800,
	(212) 563-3303
"Travel Bargains," part of the	
Travel Channel TV Network	(800) 872-8385
Travel Discounters	(800) 355-1065
(use access code "CME 7878")	
UNI Travel	(800) 325-2222,
	(314) 569-0900

from airlines fearful of not filling their planes. Initially consolidators handled only discount fares for tour groups. Now some sell to all comers at reduced prices, including your travel agent, who will, in turn, sell the ticket to you, at a slight markup.

If you are willing to forgo the niceties and security offered by a travel agent, buy directly from a consolidator. To find the names and phone numbers of consolidators, check the ads in the Sunday travel sections of *The New York Times, The Los Angeles Times,* or your local newspaper, or call those listed on this page. Although the ads are usually very small and seldom use the word consolidator, you will recognize them immediately because they offer tickets at significantly lower prices.

BEST BET ✔ Use a travel agent you trust who regularly does business with a reliable consolidator.

If you want to fly from London to Africa or the Middle or Far East, or throughout Europe, try the British version of consolidators, "bucket shops." They're centered around Earls Court Road, and ads appear in the London newspapers.

Is buying a consolidator or bucket-shop ticket safe? Usually, the price is right, and there's no advance purchase, but if you wish

DISCOUNTS FOR STUDENTS

The National Collegiate Travel Club, headquartered in New Haven, Connecticut, gives college students and their parents three certificates for last-minute travel on American or American Eagle airlines at low excursion rates. You must redeem the certificates within seventy-two hours and use them only for round-trip flights between the student's home and college or university. One of the three certificates, however, can be used for a round-trip flight between the college town and any American destination in the continental United States. Members of the Collegiate Travel Club are automatically enrolled in American's AAdvantage frequent-flyer program. Membership is $50 per year and is open to full-time undergrad and graduate students. Membership also includes a low-interest-rate credit card, discount coupons for Hertz and Alamo car rentals, and discounts on long-distance calls made with MCI. Call (800) 440-NCTC.

Another option is purchasing a Student ID Card. In addition to low airfares, this card gives students discounts on many attractions and sites around the world and in the United States plus basic sickness and accident insurance and a twenty-four-hour traveler's assistance hotline. The card costs $19 and is sponsored by the Council on International Educational Exchange. New 1997-98 benefits include:

- **Greyhound:** 15 percent off any U.S. destination
- **Club Med:** $100 off Buccaneers Resort in Martinique
- **Ski resorts:** discount in Vermont and Colorado
- **Adventure tours:** 5-10 percent off on tours
- **Yankee tickets:** 50 percent off some tickets
- **Sea World in Florida:** 10 percent off admission
- **Emergency evacuation:** up to $25,000 while overseas

For information call 888-COUNCIL, or write to Student Services, Council, 205 East 42nd Street, New York, NY 10017.

to make a change in your reservation or get a refund, it's often difficult. Ask first. Another drawback for some: You rarely know what airline you're flying on until you receive your ticket (airlines don't want it publicized that they are dealing with consolidators or bucket shops), and you may not get your ticket until the last minute.

$ TIP To be on the safe side, pay with your credit card when using a consolidator so that you'll have some recourse. If you must pay in cash, first check the consolidator's local Better Business Bureau for complaints. Confirm your flight directly with airlines. Check cancellation and exchange policies.

For a copy of *Advisory on Ticket Consolidators,* with a list of consolidators and their telephone numbers, send a check for $3.50 to Ticket Consolidators, Better Business Bureau of Metro New York, 257 Park Avenue South, New York, NY 10010.

Bucket Shops

Bucket Shop		Specialty
Benz Travel (London)	44-71-439-4181 FAX 287-9721	Germany
Bluebird Express (West Sussex)	44-444-235-678 FAX 235-789	France, Italy
Hamilton Travel (London)	44-71-344-3333 FAX 344-3347	Scandinavia
Major Travel (London)	44-71-485-7017 FAX 487-2719	Europe
Mondial Travel (London)	44-81-314-1181 FAX 314-5865	Austria, Hungary, Czech Republic
STA Travel (London)	44-71-938-4711 FAX 938-9570	Europe
Trailfinders (London)	44-71-937-5400 FAX 937-9294	Europe

FREQUENT FLYING

The frequent-flyer concept is a marketing gimmick that really took off. We all have favorite stores where we know the people who work there and we know where the merchandise is located—in short, the places we like and are comfortable with. Ditto for many products. So for the most part, we keep going to the same stores and buying the same products. In marketing this is known as "brand loyalty."

Until recently, individual airlines never knew brand loyalty. The planes are all made at the same few plants, and the personnel, for the most part, are interchangeable. Even the meals pretty much taste alike, regardless of the carrier. As a result everyone bought tickets on the basis of schedule and price.

Realizing this lack of brand loyalty, some bright person in the mid-1980s at American Airlines came up with the idea of Frequent-flyer Mileage—a way of rewarding the passenger for flying American to the exclusion of other carriers. Their frequent flyer plan said, "Look Mr. or Ms. Passenger, every time you fly American, we'll give you mileage points, which can be traded in for free trips or cabin upgrades." In effect it was a bribe to create brand loyalty—and it worked.

Within a short time every other airline got into the act. As of now, not only does every airline have a frequent-flyer plan, but so do many hotel chains and car rental firms.

One amazing fact is that only about 15 percent of all passengers redeem their frequent-flyer miles. You should be one of them.

Frequent-Flyer Strategies

Even if you don't fly on a regular basis, you can benefit from a frequent-flyer program. Here are eight tips to follow:

1. *Join as many frequent-flyer plans as possible.* There is no charge, and each airline will keep you updated on its specials, discounts, and deals. However . . .
2. *Group your miles.* It's to your advantage to accumulate as many miles as possible in one airline program rather than to have smaller amounts in several programs.

3. *Keep track of your own mileage.* Back your record up with copies of hotel, car-rental, and airline receipts to show you actually deserve the mileage. The chances that the airlines will goof in logging your miles are tremendous.

4. *Try buying points.* If you find you're a little short on bonus miles that you need for a vacation flight, you might be able to buy points from the airline. Ask.

5. *Protect yourself from an airline* that looks as though it won't be around much longer. When you have enough mileage for one or more flights, and there are rumors that the airline might fold, use the mileage immediately, or you can buy Award Guard, a type of insurance that conditionally protects your mileage from being lost; the cost is $119 for one year. Call (800) 487–8893.

6. *Get business frequent-flyer miles.* If you fly on business and your employer feels the company deserves the mileage, describe how onerous business travel really is: canceled flights, long delays, crowded airports, airline food. You undoubtedly merit keeping the mileage.

7. *Don't cash in your miles during the off-season* or when airlines are having fare wars. Wait until fares go back up.

8. *Pass on your frequent-flyer miles* to your heirs through your will, or donate them, through the airline, to charity. (There's no tax deduction, but you'll feel good.) American Airlines supports several charities through its Miles for Kids in Need program; Northwest teams up with a different nonprofit organization every quarter. Other carriers have other arrangements. Ask your travel agent or the airline.

Frequent flyers traveling on free tickets are not guaranteed the same treatment as passengers who have paid for their tickets. If the flight is delayed or canceled, the airline is less likely to endorse a frequent-flyer ticket over to another carrier; frequent flyers also are less apt to get hotel and meal vouchers. **BEST BET** ✓ Tell the gate attendant that you fly all the time; airlines don't want to lose good, steady customers.

Get Free Tickets with the Right Credit Card

By selecting one of the airline's credit cards, you can earn free air travel, even if you're not a frequent flyer. For every dollar's worth of goods you charge on an affinity card, you receive credit for mileage in a particular airline's frequent-flyer program.

In addition to American Express and Diners Club—the two big T&E (travel and entertainment) cards—seven big U.S. airlines and British Airways sponsor MasterCard or Visa cards that let you earn frequent-flyer mileage for every dollar you charge. Although these MasterCard and Visa cards are sponsored by the airlines, they are issued by banks. Most give some collision insurance on rental cars.

The T&E cards have more flexibility than the airline-sponsored cards. They don't expire, and you can use them on several airlines. With the airline cards you accrue mileage only with that particular airline and its frequent-flyer partners.

$ TIP Be aware that "frequent-flyer miles" are not necessarily actual free airline miles on a one-for-one basis. The credit can be used for free tickets, upgrades, and sometimes for vacation packages and goods.

- AMERICAN EXPRESS. AmEx's "Membership Rewards" program lets you bank earned mileage in your AmEx account and transfer credits when needed into a participating frequent-flyer program. You get 1 mile for each dollar charged on your Amex. Members must charge $5,000 to their AmEx card before mileage can be redeemed. Participants: Continental, Delta, MGM Grand, Northwest, Southwest, US Airways, Hawaiian, and their frequent-flyer partners. Call (800) 297-3276.
- DINERS CLUB. This is the only card that rewards you with frequent-flyer miles on your choice of any major U.S. airline plus a great many international ones. You earn 1 mile for every dollar you charge to the card, and you don't have to tell them up front to which frequent-flyer program you want your miles applied. When you're ready to fly, you simply call and give the information to them. Your miles do not expire,

and there's no limit to the number of miles you can earn. Or you can choose free hotel frequent-guest points or upgrades or travel packages instead of air miles. You save 20 percent on your entire restaurant bill when you eat at any one of the more than 1,700 restaurants that participate in the LeCard program. When you're away on business you have up to sixty-two days to pay your bill without interest or late fees. And if your card is lost or if you forget it, you can continue charging with a phone call to a representative. Call (800) 234-4034.

• MASTERCARD AND VISA. Airline affinity cards are issued by banks and can be used wherever Visa and MasterCard are accepted. You get frequent-flyer mileage for every dollar charged. Participants: All major U.S. airlines except Delta sponsor one or both cards.

Airline Charge Cards: Finding the Right Program

Airline	Telephone	Credit Card
Alaska	(800) 552-7302	MC, GMC, V, GV
America West	(800) 243-7762	V
American	(800) 843-0777	MC, V
Northwest	(800) 360-2900	V, GV
TWA	(800) EAB–TWA1	V, MC
United	(605) 399-2406	V, GV, GMC, MC
USAirways	(800) 282-2273	V, GV

MC = MasterCard   V = Visa
GMC = Gold MasterCard   GV = Gold Visa

Note: Annual fees and interest rates vary with the issuing company or bank.

WORKSHEET

Picking the Best Credit Card

To determine which frequent-flyer program and credit card is best for you, complete the worksheet below.

Step 1: Track your travel regularly to note which airline you fly most frequently, by filling in the worksheet below.

DATE	DESTINATION	CARRIER	FARE	HOW PAID
____	_____	____	____	_____
____	_____	____	____	_____
____	_____	____	____	_____
____	_____	____	____	_____
____	_____	____	____	_____
____	_____	____	____	_____
____	_____	____	____	_____
____	_____	____	____	_____
____	_____	____	____	_____
____	_____	____	____	_____
____	_____	____	____	_____
____	_____	____	____	_____

Step 2: Track your T&E charges to note if you meet the minimum-dollar requirement to join the frequent-flyer program by filing in the worksheet on the next page.

T&E Charges

DATE	AMERICAN EXPRESS	DINERS CLUB
_____	$_____	$_____
_____	$_____	$_____
_____	$_____	$_____
_____	$_____	$_____
_____	$_____	$_____
_____	$_____	$_____
_____	$_____	$_____
_____	$_____	$_____
_____	$_____	$_____
_____	$_____	$_____
_____	$_____	$_____
_____	$_____	$_____
Annual Total:	$_____	$_____

Step 3: Check the table on the previous page and select the card that meets your needs.

BEING BUMPED PAYS

It's a fact of life that everyone who makes a reservation doesn't show up for the flight. In airline parlance these are called "no-shows."

To counterbalance the no-shows, the airlines overbook, making reservations for more people than they can get on the flight. Sometimes, however, everyone does show up! Then the airline personnel have to get rid of the excess passenger load, which they do through something called "bumping." The gate attendant will ask passengers with confirmed reservations if they'd like to volunteer to be bumped. If chosen, they get put on the next flight and are given a voucher good for a free flight in the future, usually for anywhere in the United States that the airline flies.

$ TIP Even if you have a confirmed reservation, arrive early at the check-in gate if you want to avoid being bumped. On the other hand, if your schedule is not tight, tell the gate attendant that you want to be on the volunteer bumping list.

If your flight is canceled after you arrive at the airport, get to a pay phone and call the airline's toll-free reservation number. If you don't know it, call information, (800) 555-1212. Ask to be rebooked on the next scheduled flight to your destination. By phoning you'll avoid waiting in a long line of passengers who are also trying to rebook.

FLYING AS A COURIER

You don't need an attaché case attached to your wrist, a special password, or a trench coat to be a courier, but you do need to be

Travel Trivia

The U.S. Department of Transportation says you're least likely to be put off a flight with American Airlines—it bumps about 0.40 per 10,000 passengers. *Next best:* United, Northwest, Delta. *Worst:* Continental, America West, Southwest.

Air-Courier Brokers

Now Voyager	(212) 431-1616
Discount Travel	(212) 362-3636
Courier Travel	(516) 763-6898
Way To Go	(213) 466-1126

flexible and willing to travel light. If you fulfill these requirements, you can fly to many foreign destinations for about half price by acting as an escort for parcels: financial papers, architectural drawings, manuscripts, etc.

Using ordinary citizens as couriers evolved as a way to solve the problem the air freight companies face. These companies promise to get parcels to foreign countries by next-day or second-day air. If they send them with their regular air-freight shipment, it takes several days to clear customs. Their solution: to use air couriers—you.

In exchange for a reduced fare (about 50 percent off), you agree to fly with only carry-on luggage and give up your checked luggage space to the company, which uses it for its packages. You seldom see the items involved, but it's all legitimate stuff. A representative from the courier company will meet you at the airport and make all the arrangements for handling the parcels. That's it. They get their stuff delivered, and you get cheap airfare.

Air couriers fly from New York, Los Angeles, Miami, Houston, and San Francisco. Some air-courier brokers charge a membership fee ($50–$100) and/or a refundable deposit. To find out about getting tickets, call those listed here. Be prepared to do a lot of phoning. You may also want to subscribe to the following newsletter for more information and listings, plus details on last-minute flights: *Shoestring Traveler,* Box 1349, Lake Worth, FL 33460 (407-582-8320). It's published by the International Association of Air Couriers, and costs $45 per year.

$ TIP The closer to departure time, the cheaper the ticket. Some couriers have gotten free tickets by being able to leave at the last minute.

TAKING CHARTER FLIGHTS

Here's yet another way to get rock-bottom fares—sometimes. Charter operators fly from some forty U.S. and Canadian cities to popular vacation spots and major cities around the world. They tend to be seasonally oriented; that is, in the winter most go from a northern city to a warmer spot, with Mexico and the Caribbean being extremely popular. Most undercut the lowest fares on scheduled airlines, and most sell all seats at the same price. Many run only one trip weekly, and it's tough to get a refund or exchange your ticket. (For a list of leading charter operators, see the table on the next page.)

$ TIP Charters are not always your cheapest bet. Before buying a ticket, check Continental and USAirways, which have low-fare flights, as well as any new start-up lines. During fare wars, regularly scheduled lines may actually undercut charters. The difference between a charter flight and a regularly scheduled one has to do with contracts: With a charter your contract is with a tour operator, not an airline. The tour operator actually charters a plane and crew from the airline that then operates the flight. This distinction is not critical unless things go wrong; then it's up to the tour operator to fix it, not the airline. Consequently, travelers have been left stranded because the tour operator went out of business and the airline was never paid for the return flight.

Charters usually don't sell seats directly to the public or list fares, schedules, and seat availability in the computerized systems used by travel agencies, although there are some exceptions. Not all travel agents keep up with the charters; in fact, some don't sell them at all.

Charters serve very limited areas, and usually do not make connecting flights. In other words they go from one major city to another or from a major city to a popular vacation spot.

CAUTION Don't be misled by the word *scheduled*. Charters do adhere to a schedule. *Scheduled* airlines are the majors, such as American, United, etc., but a handful of small airlines operate scheduled service under charter rules. Starting up a charter line involves less red tape than starting a scheduled line.

You should know that airlines are licensed by the government to provide scheduled flights and to sell tickets on them. On the

Leading Charter Operators

Balair	(800) 322-5247	(212) 581-3411
Council Charter	(800) 800-8222	(212) 661-0311
Fantasy Holidays	(800) 645-2555	(516) 935-8500
Homeric Tours	(800) 223-5570	(212) 753-1100
Martinair Holland	(800) 366-4655	(561) 391-6165
New Frontiers	(800) 677-0720	(310) 670-7302
SunTrips	(800) 786-8747	(408) 432-1101
Travel Charter	(800) 521-5267	(810) 641-9677

other hand, airlines or charter operators can sell an entire flight to a single club or group. This is called an affinity charter. Or they can sell charter seats to individual travelers, which is called a public charter. Public charters are governed more tightly by the Department of Transportation than are affinity charters. The money paid for a charter ticket must be held in an escrow account and not released until after the trip is over. If you buy directly from the operator, your check should be made out to the escrow bank. If you are using a travel agent, the travel agent deducts his or her commission and also sends a check to the bank. The purpose behind this is to safeguard the money should the operator fail or the trip not be made, and then the money will be refunded.

CAUTION ☞ These rules apply to cash and checks and do not cover the use of credit cards to pay for public-charter tickets.

HOW TO GO STANDBY

One agency, Airhitch, has a standby program for charters to Europe. You give Airhitch a five-day time period in which you wish to leave, with your desired destination and one or two alternative destinations. You must pay in advance, and you'll find out a few days ahead of time when you leave and to which city you'll be flying. Return plans are made in a similar fashion through a European-affiliated office. For information call (212) 864-2000.

DIRECTORY OF SMALL CARRIERS

Carrier	Began Service	Sample Destinations	Hub City
Air South (800) 247-7688	1994	Atlanta; Columbia, S.C.; Miami; Charlotte; Tampa/St. Petersburg	Columbia, S.C.
American Trans Air (800) 225-9919	1981	Las Vegas; Chicago; Indianapolis; Milwaukee; Cancun	Indianapolis
Carnival (800) 824-7386	1988	Bahamas; Caribbean; Florida; Northeast; Puerto Rico	Ft. Lauderdale
Frontier (800) 432-1359	1944	Denver; Montana; N. Dakota; Phoenix; Los Angeles	Denver
Kiwi (800) 538-5494	1992	Atlanta; Chicago; Newark; San Juan; Tampa/St. Petersburg; West Palm Beach	Newark
Midway Airlines (800) 446-4392	1993	Chicago to Dallas; Denver; New York; Philadelphia; Washington, D.C.	Raleigh/Durham
Reno Air (800) 736-6247	1992	Reno; San Jose; Los Angeles; Seattle; and all over the West Coast	Reno
Southwest (800) 435-9792	1993	Los Angeles; Chicago; San Francisco	Phoenix; Dallas
Spirit Airlines (800) 772-7117	1992	East Coast; Florida; Detroit; Atlantic City	Detroit
Sun Jet Int'l (800) 478-6538	1993	Dallas; Long Beach, Calif.; Newark; Tampa/St. Petersburg; West Palm Beach; Orlando	Newark
Tower Air (800) 348-6937 (718) 553-8500	1983	Miami; Los Angeles; San Francisco; seven foreign cities from New York, including Tel Aviv	New York
Valujet (800) 825-8538	1993	Atlanta; Washington, D.C.;Orlando; Tampa	Atlanta

SMALL CARRIERS

There are many smaller carriers that are perfectly safe. The general public, however, usually doesn't know of them because they don't have extensive advertising budgets. It pays to know about them because they fly to less popular destinations and to rural areas. Also, you may find their prices attractive.

AIRLINE PROBLEMS

Lost Luggage

One out of every 200 bags checked is reported lost. More luggage is lost in December, January, and February than at other times of the year. Airlines that most often lose bags are Continental and USAirways; those that lose the fewest bags are Southwest, American, and America West. To find out how airlines score on baggage handling, call the Department of Transportation at (202) 366-2220.

Airline policies vary, but in general, here's what to do when your luggage doesn't show up.

1. Fill out a complaint form while you're still at the airport. Wait twenty-four hours for results. (Be sure an airline employee signs the form.)
2. If your luggage does not show up, you can get an allowance of $25 to $50. To claim it, you must return to the airport.
3. After forty-eight hours you're entitled to another $25 for emergency supplies; bring receipts from your purchases.
4. Bags never found? The maximum you're entitled to is $1,250 no matter how many bags you had. And that's for depreciated value, not original value, which is why we recommend that you always make a detailed list of what you've packed plus a record of the cost of your bags themselves. And remember, an airline can deny coverage completely for fragile and perishable items that you've packed.
5. Check your homeowner's insurance policy and your credit card coverage to see if you can get more.
6. You may want to purchase extra coverage at the airport—it generally runs 50 cents to $2.00 per $100 extra coverage.

Lost Tickets

Getting a replacement or refund for a lost ticket will be difficult and time consuming—count on it. The airlines are worried about fraudulent claims and so they "encourage" you to be extra careful. That translates into the fact that you may have to pay a fee of up to $50 if you lose your ticket. And, believe it or not, if your ticket is found and used by someone else, *your refund request may be denied!*

To protect yourself, buy your tickets with a credit card so you have absolute proof of purchase. Then think of your tickets as cash and know where they are at all times. If you do lose them, report the fact at once to the airline or travel agent.

Airline Strikes

If you're booked on an airline that goes on strike, what can you expect? The answer, unfortunately, is very little. Airlines don't care too much that your vacation had to be canceled, that you couldn't get to an important meeting, or that you were stranded with two children for hours at the airport.

If you've made your reservation through a travel agent, he or she will work very hard to get you on the next available flight. That is, if the strike or flight cancelation takes place during regular business hours when you can reach your agent. And, of course, calling your agent means access to information on all airlines—which is a lot easier than dialing a batch of 800 numbers from a pay phone. If you hold a frequent-flyer ticket or have purchased your ticket from a consolidator, other airlines may not accept it.

Be smart and keep a photocopy of your ticket, ticket number, itinerary, credit card receipt, and photo ID separate from your ticket. Sometimes, if you discover your ticket is lost at the last minute, the airline may let you board without insisting that you purchase another ticket if you have a photocopy of all of the above.

Labor strikes fall into the same category as "Act of God" and "Act of War," which means there's no legal requirement for the airline to help out the consumer. Airlines are not required to compensate passengers when their flights are canceled or delayed. They are only required to provide compensation to passengers bumped from an overbooked flight.

$ TIP When you hear news of an impending strike at an airline on which you have booked a ticket, call your travel agent. Book refundable tickets on alternative carriers. Then, if your original carrier takes off, the backup ticket can be cashed in.

Death or Injury

If the worst happens and you or someone in your immediate family is injured or killed in an airplane accident, be sure to get a copy of the book *After the Crash*. It's free to next of kin and injured passengers ($10 for anyone else) from HALT, 1319 F Street, NW (Suite 300), Washington, DC 20004; (202) 347–9600.

Registering a Complaint

If you have any complaints about an airline and would like to take action, contact the Office of Consumer Affairs, U.S. Department of Transportation (DOT), 400 Seventh Street SW, Room 10405, Washington, DC 20590; (202) 366–2220.

1. Put your complaint in writing. Stick to the point. Keep it short.
2. Enclose copies (not originals) of tickets, receipts, etc.
3. State if you're a member of the airline's frequent-flyer club.
4. State the solution you're seeking.
5. Add something positive about a staff person; you'll be taken more seriously than if you're just a complainer.
6. Send a copy to the airline's customer-service department.

HANDLING JET LAG

Left alone, jet lag (extreme drowsiness, insomnia, waking at crazy hours, and other odd feelings that occur when you cross too many time zones in a short period) slowly diminishes, although some effects can last as long as twelve days. It can be a real nuisance and, for the business traveler, a disaster. There have been all kinds of remedies suggested over the years. Some seem to work for some people. These are worth trying:

1. Eat lightly on the plane.
2. Avoid liquor and caffeine.
3. Walk about the cabin every two hours.
4. Wear loose-fitting clothes.
5. Drink water every few hours.
6. A week before departure, if you're traveling east, get up an hour earlier each day and have meals an hour earlier daily until, by the end of the week, you're rising at 2:00 A.M. and having dinner at 2:00 P.M.
7. Get a free copy of "The Argonne Anti-Jet Lag Diet" from: Office of Public Affairs, Argonne National Laboratories, 9700 South Cass Avenue, Argonne, IL 60439; (708) 252–5575.
8. For a free copy of the pamphlet *Defeating Jet Lag,* send a stamped, self-addressed business-sized envelope to The Forsyth Travel Library, Box 480800, Kansas City, MO 64148.

BEING SAFE

A question we're asked all the time is, "What's the safest part of the plane?" Repeated accident reports indicate that fatalities can occur anywhere, depending on how the accident occurs and the configuration of the aircraft. On the other hand, there is a premium to getting out of a damaged plane at once to avoid ensuing explosions, smoke, fumes, or fire. To exit quickly, sit next to an exit door, or if that's not possible, carefully note where the exits are and be prepared to get to one of them in an emergency. Mentally rehearse what you would do.

Smoke hoods, which you slip over your head in an emergency, protect against smoke and heat and have a clear visor that helps you see in smoky areas. Folded, the hoods are about the size of a man's handkerchief and sell for about $70 from Magellan's. To order call (800) 962–4943.

Sky Safety

According to the University of California at Berkeley's "Wellness Letter," if you flew in a commercial airline to random airports in the United States every single day of your life, it would take a mind-boggling average of 26,000 years before you would be killed in a crash.

Since 1989, the number of airline departures has grown from 7.6 million to more than 8 million, while accidents per million departures have dropped from 3.66 to 2.86. USAirways has had more accidents than any other major U.S. airlines since 1989, but with more flights than most, its accident rate is actually lower than many.

The Federal Aviation Administration keeps a list of airlines worldwide that do not meet international safety standards. A "conditional" rating means that the airline may fly into the United States, but only under more severe FAA surveillance. The FAA also has a list of carriers that are not allowed to send any planes to the United States. To check up on an airline, call the FAA's hotline at (800) 322–7873.

Airline	Accidents	Accident Rate Per Million Flights
USAirways	14	2.6
American	12	2.5
United	12	3.1
Delta	10	1.9
Continental	9	3.4
America West	5	4.3
Northwest	3	1.0
TWA	2	1.3
Southwest	2	0.9

(*Note:* "Accidents" involve death or serious passenger injury. *Source:* National Transportation Safety Board and FAA data.)

The 1997 *Airport Transit Guide* lists ways to get to the nearest city from more 400 airports around the world. It also covers wheelchair access, trip times, and rental car companies. It costs $8.95. Contact Magellan's, (800) 962-4943.

The critical times: takeoff and landing. That's why you're asked to keep your seat belt buckled. Don't be macho. Do it.

Another safety measure: Read the safety instructions in the seatback pocket every single time you fly, no matter how "square" it may seem. Each plane has different instructions.

EATING WHILE ALOFT

Airline food is considered by many to be an oxymoron. In first class or business class, however, the choice and the food itself are usually quite good. In coach, considering that a handful of cabin attendants are trying to feed hundreds within a short period of time, it's surprising when it's not a culinary disaster. At times it is.

TIP   Bring your own large coffee mug. You'll get more, and it will stay warm longer.

Even in coach, you can avoid ordinary airline cuisine and have healthful, appealing food by ordering a special meal, at no extra charge, when you make your reservation. United has the greatest selection of special meals—more than twenty, including seafood and fruit plates, Kosher, Hindu, and Muslim meals, or a chef's salad.

AIRLINE CLUBS

If you travel often with a particular airline, you might want to consider joining its club. Check first to see if your credit card already provides access to an airport club. For example, American Express Platinum Card lets you into Continental and Northwest lounges when flying those airlines, and Diners Club has sixty-four airport lounges just for its cardholders.

Airline clubs charge a onetime entrance fee that can range from $25 to $100 plus an annual fee. Some let you pay with frequent-flyer miles; some offer spousal memberships, lifetime membership, longer-term memberships. A couple of clubs have one-day passes. Most let you bring in a guest.

What do you get? Quiet, comfort, fax machines, computers, printers, snacks, TV, magazines, telephones, copiers, maybe even a conference room, clean restrooms, showers. You can also use a club to receive messages or meet someone. In most cases, a ticket agent in the club will handle seat assignments, issue boarding passes, and help you change reservations, so there's no standing in line at the gate or public ticket counter. And, if your flight is either canceled or delayed, you're more apt to get a good seat on the next flight. Club ticket agents are also adept at getting upgrades for members.

The world's best lounge, say many, is Virgin Atlantic's at Heathrow, which comes with virtual ski machines; a music room with CDs; a 5,000-volume library; a salon with free massages, manicures, and hairstyling; a four-hole putting green; and more. If you can, check out the lounge in the airport(s) you use most often before signing on. See if it has what you want.

Airline Clubs

Airline	Annual Fee	Number of Clubs
Alaska	$150	7
American	$200	46
America West	$150	2
Continental	$150	16
Delta	$200	45
Northwest	$195	30
TWA	$150	24
United	$175+	44
USAirways	$175	30

3

RIDING THE RAILS: TRAIN TRAVEL

WITH NOTES ON BUS TRAVEL

> *To travel by train is to see nature and human beings, towns and churches and rivers, in fact to see life.*
>
> — *Agatha Christie*

AGATHA CHRISTIE knew that speed isn't everything. Along with it come crowded airports, flight delays, cancellations, small seats, and squished legs. Trains, on the other hand, are conveniently located in city centers, so there's none of the hassle and expense involved in going to and from an airport, and there's plenty of legroom to accommodate the tallest basketball player. Riding the rails is also relaxing. You can sit in a wide-windowed coach or in your own compartment and watch the countryside roll by, with no traffic, turbulence, or much thought given to the weather, and anxiety about making connections is pretty much eliminated. Best of all, there's plenty of uninterrupted time in which to work, read, rest, dream.

TRAVEL ON AMTRAK

Amtrak, which took over the nation's passenger rail network in 1971, has been continually upgrading its service, but that, of course, doesn't mean all trains provide equally good service. They don't. The trick to a successful ride is to know which train to take and what type of accommodation to book.

Amtrak Travel Tips

Here are fourteen ways to make riding the rails work for you.

1. *For overnights, go first class,* unless you don't mind sitting up all night; if you don't mind, you'll save a bundle. Meals, but not liquor, are included in the price of all first-class tickets. It's very important to understand the space you're buying. For example, east of the Mississippi, a *roomette* for one person has a wide armchair for day travel, a toilet and sink, plus a pull-out bed, all in one room. When lying in bed you can look out the window. A *bedroom* has either two armchairs or one sofa as well as two beds that fold out of the walls, plus a separate bathroom. The upper bed is higher than the window, so the person in the upper bed cannot look out at the landscape. West of the Mississippi, sleepers are newer and have larger bedrooms. The *deluxe bedroom* has a sofa and a swivel chair, two beds, toilet, and shower, whereas a *family bedroom* has even more room. Before booking ask Amtrak to show or send you a diagram of the various sleeping accommodations offered.

   TIP A perk of first-class travel: You can use the special Amtrak "Metropolitan Lounges" in a handful of cities. They are attractive and safe and have comfortable sofas, chairs, writing desks, telephones, faxes, free coffee, tea, cold beverages, reading material, and helpful attendants. You can stow your bags there while waiting, and just before departure a porter will take them from the lounge and deliver them to your train seat.

2. *Bathroom needs must be taken into consideration* when booking a sleeper. If you use the bathroom during the night, you'll

need a compartment in which the toilet is not under the bed when the bed is pulled down. On most Amtrak trains the bedrooms have a separate, private bathroom, so you won't need to fold up your bed to use the facilities; in a roomette, however, the toilet is under the folded-down bed. In some smaller roomettes, the toilet is on the side of the folded-down bed. *Ask.* Solution: Take a robe so that you can walk to a car where there is a general bathroom.

3. *Laptop users in sleeping compartments* can get a table that hooks into the wall. Bring your own very long extension cord—in many sleeping compartments, the only electric outlet is in the bathroom, too far away for a computer's standard cord to reach. **CAUTION** ☛ Trains frequently enter blackout periods, so sensitive computers should be run on batteries. Also, pack a three- to two-prong plug and vice versa because outlets are not uniform.

4. *Overnight coach travelers* should bring their own blanket and pillow. Although available (often for a small fee) on most routes, these creature comforts are often in short supply.

5. *Bring your own reading material,* map, playing cards, writing paper, stamps, pen. Headphones are required for Walkmans, Watchmans, and radios.

6. *Ask the conductor for Amtrak route guides* as soon as you board. These useful brochures have detailed maps that highlight key points of interest to look at from both sides of the train. They're available on all long routes.

7. *Get the current issue of Amtrak's* America, a magazine that describes the major trains, their routes (with maps), and equipment, as well as details on vacation packages, escorted rail tours, and a list of hotels where Amtrak passengers get reduced rates. Call (800) USA-RAIL for a free copy.

8. *Check out discounts.* In conjunction with United Express, Amtrak now serves eighty-six U.S. cities with a rail trip one way and an airline flight the other—at one price. There are also discounts for kids ages two to fifteen, and for seniors over age sixty-two. United Airlines Mileage Plus members get credit for the air portion of the trip. For information call Amtrak's Great American Vacations at (800)

321–8684. Periodically Amtrak gives 55 percent off one-way fares if the fare costs $75 or more, so ask if there's an "Amtrak Meets You More Than Half Way" fare when booking (not available on Metroliner or auto trains).

9. *Go coach.* Check out the "All Aboard America" rates. Amtrak has divided the United States into three major geographical areas. With this plan you can stop off three times with each pass. The plan costs $140 for travel within one region, $180 for two regions, and $225 for all three regions. For example, you can go from New York to Los Angeles, stop off in three cities in three different areas, and then ride back to New York for just $225. The passes are not good in peak seasons and are nonrefundable. Children ages two to fifteen go half price, and seniors age sixty-two and older get a 15 percent discount. Call (800) USA–RAIL.

10. *Save more money.* Stay at hotels within walking distance (or a short bus or taxi ride) of train stations, and make the longest train trips during the night, when fares are lower.

11. *Tell your age.* If you're sixty-two or over, you can get a 15 percent discount off the lowest available rail fare every day of the week, but not during Christmas/New Year's or on Metroliners or auto trains at any time. The lowest round-trip rail fares usually sell out quickly, so book well in advance. (See the table below for recent sample fares.)

12. *Use the club car on Metroliner service* between major East Coast cities, especially if you're traveling during mealtime.

Sample Amtrak Fares

Route	Regular Fare	Fare for Persons Age 62 and Over
Los Angeles–Chicago	$198	$168
New York–Chicago	141	120
New York–Washington	120	102
Los Angeles–San Francisco	84	72

You won't save money; in fact, you'll need a first-class ticket, but you will get more privacy and legroom, and meals (delivered to your seat) are included in the price. There are single seats on one side of the aisle and two seats on the opposite side.

13. *Ask about special fares*—weekend fares, one-week fares, one-month fares, tours, seasonal discounts, and round-trip savings—not only in the United States but also abroad. For example, a one-way Metroliner ticket between New York and Philadelphia is $58 on weekdays, but a round-trip excursion is only $39 and takes just fifteen minutes longer.

14. *Be realistic about the food.* Don't expect a gourmet experience. Quality and dining facilities vary considerably. Dining cars on some routes have linen tablecloths and china, whereas others use plastic for everything. Food is seldom prepared to order, so stick with sensible choices that microwave well: chicken, hamburger, omelets, pasta. Have cocktails in your room or the club car; dining-car space is limited, and a leisurely drink before eating is not always feasible. The "house," or "train," wine is invariably excellent on all Amtrak trains.

Amtrak Update: The West Coast

The famous *Coast Starlight,* operating daily between Los Angeles and Seattle, has been upgraded, and, if the service doesn't meet your expectations, you'll receive a credit toward another one-way trip. The food is prepared by chefs trained at culinary institutes and includes fresh pastries, seafood, and wine tastings. There are movies and a children's play area with board games, books, videos,

Amtrak now has a frequent-rider incentive program aboard Metroliner trains. It's called "Executive Privileges Program." With every two round-trip Metroliner rides you get a free upgrade to first class, free Transmedia Discount Dining Card, and 20 percent off at certain hotels. Call (800) 836–6656.

Insider's Tip

Maintaining Your Privacy: If you're not in the mood for a conversation with your seatmate on a train, plane, or bus, wear headphones, even if you're not listening to the music. You'll be less likely to be disturbed by a talkative fellow traveler.

---

and stuffed animals. During the day, watch the spectacular scenery through wraparound picture windows in the sightseeing lounge car. Fare includes five full meals. (800) USA-RAIL.

Amtrak Update: The East Coast

Amtrak has finally seen the light . . . and so will you with the new Viewliners on the East Coast corridor to Miami, from Boston, New York, Philadelphia, Washington, D.C., and other major cities. The tiny, claustrophobic sleeping cars of the past have been replaced with spacious Viewliners. Now you can enjoy decent headroom, comfortable seating, legroom, overhead baggage storage above the aisle, and two sets of windows so the person in the upper berth can look outside. Viewliners also have brighter lights, in-room climate controls, two music channels, and a small video screen with two movies per trip.

The Standard Viewliner measures 6½ x 3½ feet and has two reclining seats (which combine into a lower berth) and an upper berth that pulls out of the wall. There's a toilet with a fold-down top that doubles as a nightstand and a fold-up sink. There's also a tidy, fold-away table for cards, in-room dining, or writing. The Deluxe Viewliner measures 6½ x 7½ feet and has an armchair and a sofa. The sofa converts into the lower berth; the upper berth folds out of the wall. There's a separate toilet and shower.

Rates vary; if you book well in advance you may get a discount. If you're sixty-two or older, you get a 15 percent discount off the basic fare. Leave on a Monday, Tuesday, or Wednesday and you'll get additional discounts because weekends are peak travel times. For information call (800) 872-7245.

GREAT U.S. & CANADIAN TRAIN RIDES

Amtrak Journeys

There are a number of spectacular Amtrak routes that showcase the great diversity and grandeur of the United States. Book well in advance for these six popular trains. For reservations call (800) USA–RAIL.

- *ADIRONDACK* (New York to Montreal). A lovely trip up the Hudson River, through the Adirondacks, with a view of Lake Champlain and the St. Lawrence River and Seaway as you pull into Montreal. **BEST BET** Sit on the left side (the river side) when leaving Manhattan. At Albany switch to the right, or east side.
- *CALIFORNIA ZEPHYR* (Chicago to Oakland via Denver and Salt Lake City). See the Rocky Mountains and the Colorado River, and pass through the sheer-walled Glenwood Canyon. The train goes through the 6-mile Moffat Tunnel beneath the Continental Divide (rivers on the east side flow to the Atlantic Ocean and on the west side to the Pacific Ocean). You'll also go through the Sierra Mountains and Donner Pass. **BEST BET** Take the trip heading west because the most interesting stretch is crossing the Rockies out of Denver, which you'll do in the daylight.
- *CAPITOL LIMITED* (Washington, D.C., to Chicago). Winds up the Potomac River and through the Appalachians. Between Pittsburgh and Washington, D.C., the train follows the old Baltimore & Ohio line through some of the prettiest scenery in the East.
- *CARDINAL* (Chicago to Washington, D.C.). Goes along the Ohio River, twisting through the Blue Ridge Moutains and the Appalachians, cutting through the dramatic New River Gorge.
- *COAST STARLIGHT* (Seattle to Los Angeles). Speeds along the West Coast, known for its sheer cliffs and dazzling drops to the ocean. You'll see the Pacific Palisades, the Cascade Mountains, and Puget Sound. **BEST BET** Head north to capture the most daylight.

- *PIONEER* (Chicago to Seattle). This is part of the *California Zephyr* train until Salt Lake City, where it branches off and then climbs through the Blue Mountains, on to the Columbia River and to Portland. The last lap is along the Cascade Range to Seattle.

Excursion Railroads

The following railroad companies offer short, scenic trips and run primarily in the spring/summer/fall, with some special Thanksgiving and holiday-time excursions.

In the East:
- Strasburg Rail Co., Box 96, Strasburg, PA 17597; (717) 687–7522
- East Broad Top Railroad, Rockhill Furnace, PA 17249; (814) 447–3011
- Valley Railroad Co., Box 452, Essex, CT 06426; (860) 767–0103

In the West:
- Durango & Silverton Narrow-Gauge Railroad, 479 Main Avenue, Durango, CO 81301; (970) 247–2733

In the South:
- Cass Scenic Railroad State Park, Box 107, Cass, WV 24927; (304) 456–4300

Canadian Train Trip

Rail Canada runs a special train called the *Chaleur,* which consists of recently restored 1950s vintage cars. There are two sleepers, a coach car, and a domed lounge/diner.

It leaves Montreal's Central Station at 7:00 P.M. several times a week. After it crosses the St. Lawrence River, you're served cocktails and dinner (linen tablecloths, fresh flowers, great food, china). By the time the train pulls into Quebec, you'll probably be in bed. Around sunrise the train stops at Matapedia, where it splits into two sections: the Halifax-bound *Ocean* and the Gaspe-bound *Chaleur.* From there you'll wind through countryside, along beaches, and through forests. Breakfast is served starting at

6:30 A.M. At 11:10 you arrive in Gaspe. Departure back to
Montreal is at 3:50 P.M. with arrival the next morning.
   For information call Via Rail Canada, (800) 561–3949.

FALL FOLIAGE BY RAIL

Most of us see autumn's blaze of color from a car or bus window,
yet leaf-peeping by train completely eliminates all the hassle of
highway and back-road traffic jams. For more information contact Amtrak in summer, long before the leaves begin to turn.

- *NORTHEAST.* The best color is on the route between New
  Haven and Boston, which parallels the Atlantic shoreline,
  and on Empire Service trains, which leave New York City for
  Albany, Montreal, or Niagara Falls. The tracks run right
  alongside the Hudson River. **BEST BET** ✅ The best rides are
  on the *Adirondack* (see above) and the *Maple Leaf*—the latter
  continues west to Buffalo, Niagara Falls, and Toronto.
- *MID-ATLANTIC.* The trains between Philadelphia and
  Harrisburg go through Pennsylvania Dutch country.
  BEST BET ✅ The *Pennsylvanian* and the eastbound
  Broadway Limited have great views of the Allegheny
  Mountains. (Book on the Keystone Classic Club, a luxurious
  lounge car attached to the *Pennsylvanian.*) Amtrak's triweekly
  Cardinal has spectacular views of the Skyline Drive in the
  Blue Ridge Mountains.
- *SOUTHEAST.* Take Amtrak's *Crescent* through the Virginia
  foothills and Piedmont area of Georgia. The *Carolinian* has
  superb views on the northbound run.
- *MIDWEST.* Any train from Chicago to Michigan is worth rid-
  ing. In Michigan Amtrak offers a hotel package at
  Dearborn's Best Western/Greenfield Inn. There are good
  views also on the route between St. Louis and Kansas City,
  Missouri, with a special stop at Hermann, Missouri, during
  its five "Oktoberfest" weekends.
- *WEST.* Heading west from Chicago, the *Empire Builder* travels
  through brilliant colors in Wisconsin and Minnesota and
  along the Mississippi River. The *California Zephyr* (see above)

> ## Amtrak Ski Packages
>
> Amtrak ski packages include round-trip coach fare, lodging, resort amenities, lift tickets, and free transfers from the Amtrak train station to the front door of the resort. Accommodations range from well-known luxury resorts to family-style condos, with double-occupancy prices going from about $295 to $465 per person for three nights up to $600 per person for five nights.
>
> - For Ski Amtrak packages in New Mexico and Colorado, call: RMA Travel & Tours at (800) 841–9800.
> - For packages in Utah, call Sports America Tours at (800) 876–8551.
> - For packages at Lake Placid, New York, and at Killington and Stowe, Vermont, call Go Go Tours at (800) 899–2558.
> - With Amtrak's AirRail Travel Plan, in conjunction with United Airlines, you can travel by rail with stopovers and return by air. For information call (800) 321–8684.

passes through Aspen's yellow foliage and the flaming reds in the Rocky Mountains.

RIDING THE RAILS TO THE SLOPES

Toss out the ice scrapers and tire chains; instead, ride the rails to the trails. Amtrak lets you check your skis when boarding and retrieve them at your destination, or you can bring them aboard as carry-on luggage when checked baggage service is not available. Amtrak not only has trains that stop at the country's leading ski resorts, but it also has a number of well-priced packaged tours. (See Amtrak Ski Packages above.)

- *NORTHEAST.* The *Vermonter,* which travels between Washington, D.C., and Montreal, stops at White River Junction for Woodstock and Killington; at Essex Junction for Bolton Valley and Smugglers' Notch; at Waterbury-Stowe for Sugarbush and Stowe; and at St. Albans for Jay Peak.

- *MID-ATLANTIC.* The Chicago–New York *Broadway Limited* and the Chicago–Washington, D.C., *Capitol Limited* make stops in Pittsburgh near Seven Springs and Hidden Valley resorts. The *Capitol Limited* also stops in Cumberland, Maryland, near Wisp.

- *WEST.* The *Southwest Chief* from Los Angeles has a stop in Flagstaff for the Fairfield Snowbowl and in Lamy, New Mexico, for Taos and Santa Fe ski resorts. The *Pioneer* stops at Rock Springs for Jackson Hole skiing. On the *Empire Builder* you can train it to Big Mountain in Whitefish, Montana; Schweitzer in Sandpoint, Idaho; and other ski areas in Washington state.

The *California Zephyr,* which runs between Chicago and San Francisco, stops in Denver for shuttle service to Breckenridge, Copper Mountain, Arapahoe Basin, Keystone, Vail, and Beaver Creek. Then, west of Denver, the *Zephyr* stops at Winter Park. From the Salt Lake City stop, skiers can reach Park City, Alta/Snowbird, and Brighton/Solitude.

WESTERN TRAIN TOURS

There are three interesting rides—a Rockies Tour, a Yellowstone Tour, and a Continental Divide Tour—ranging in price from about $400 to $2,000 per person double occupancy. These trains depart from Spokane, Washington, and Billings, Montana, and range from three to five nights, staying overnight in hotels. Pre- and post-tour hotel nights available at reasonable rates. For information call Montana Rockies Rail Tours, (800) 519-RAIL.

The Skunk Train, departing from Fort Bragg, California, traverses the famous Redwood Route originally laid out in 1855—in fact, it's a 40-mile trip back into American history, along the scenic Noyo River north to its final destination of Willits. For information call (707) 964-6371.

EUROPEAN TRAIN TRAVEL

It's easy to speed through Europe riding the rails—in style, safety, and comfort. Trains on some of the new high-tech tracks now average 130 to 170 miles per hour. Depending on how many places you'll be visiting, it may pay to buy a rail pass and get unlimited travel over a certain number of days rather than individual train tickets.

The most comprehensive of the passes is the Eurailpass, which lets you ride on the major national rails of seventeen Western European countries (but not Great Britain) and Hungary. With a full-time Eurailpass, you can travel on any day during the time period. With a flexible pass you can travel on only a certain number of days within the overall time period. For example, with a five-day/two-month pass, you can travel on any five days during a two-month period. The Eurailpass also lets you travel either free or at a discount on some suburban trains (but not on city transit systems), private railways, national buses, ferries, and excursion boats.

Here are some general recommendations:

1. *A Eurailpass is best* for extended, multicountry travel. If you're just going to one country, then a national or regional pass is a better bet.
2. *A flexible pass is cheaper* than a full-time pass, but you must keep your train travel within a limited number of days.
3. *If you're staying in only one city* or perhaps just two, buy a separate ticket for any intercity trip(s).
4. *A rail/car pass* is a good deal if you're combining a long train trip with just one-day auto trips. On the other hand, if you're going to do a lot of driving, you'll be better off to go with a weekly car rental. A car is also more economical for two or more people traveling together.
5. *Fly if you're going to only a few cities* that are far apart.

Following are various passes that are now available. A number of these passes give discounts to senior citizens, who can buy individual tickets at discounted rates in many countries, often at 50 percent off.

- Regional passes, available for Benelux (Belgium, Luxembourg, and the Netherlands) and Scandinavia (Denmark, Finland, Norway, and Sweden), are cheaper than the Eurailpass, especially in second class.
- The European East pass is good for Austria, the Czech Republic, Hungary, Poland, and Slovakia. The Central Europe pass covers the Czech Republic, Germany, Poland, and Slovakia.
- Other regional passes: BritIreland (Britain, the Republic, Ulster, and the Irish Sea ferry), BritFrance, and BritGermany.

Is first class worth it? It's generally sold at a premium of 50 percent (versus as much as 500 percent on airlines) and gives you much more spacious seating areas as well as meal service. On long trips during the high season, when second class is invariably jammed, it's worth it.

THE *ORIENT EXPRESS* AND OTHER LUXURY TRAINS

If you like to travel in the manner favored by royalty, Isadora Duncan, and Mata Hari, the *Orient Express* is the ideal trip. After indulging the whims and fancies of the wealthy for nearly one hundred years, the *Orient Express* ground to a halt in 1977. In 1982, the born-again train resumed service from London to Venice. The train runs once a week, with a morning departure from Victoria Station. After a two-hour ride to Folkstone, passengers board the Sea Link British Ferry for a ninety-minute trip to Boulogne, France. In Boulogne sleeping cars are assigned. The train goes through France and the Swiss Alps before arriving in Venice. The trip takes thirty-two hours, with the nighttime portion occurring between Paris and Zurich; you'll have more than twenty daylight hours in which to

If you want to sample the trip but not pay the full price, you can purchase day seats on these segments: London to Paris, $715; Zurich to Venice, $810; Zurich to Innsbruck, $625; Innsbruck to Venice, $530.

enjoy spectacular scenery. Passengers may stop over in Paris, Zurich, St. Anton, Innsbruck, or Verona for an additional fee of $225 per stopover on the southbound journey. Return-trip arrangements must be scheduled in advance. At the present time northbound stopovers are free. The current fare from London to Venice, including cabin and dinner, is $1,785 per person, double occupancy. If you book round-trip, the discounted fare is $2,590. Singles pay an additional $300 one way and $435 round-trip.

Most of the London-to-Venice trains have seventeen carriages—ten are sleeping cars, three are for dining, and one is for drinking and listening to a piano player. Cabins have been restored to their original elegance; you'll have a washstand but no private toilet—those are at the end of the carriage, so take a robe and slippers. There are no showers. **TIP** Try to book an air-conditioned car (not all are) and one of the first or last cars. These are quieter and more private because fewer passengers walk through them on their way to the dining and drinking cars.

Men will need a dark suit and necktie; in fact, nearly half the men on board wear black tie. Women can dress to the nines; many wear long dresses from the 1920s and 1930s.

There's also a new sister train from Singapore to Bangkok. The *Eastern Orient Express* leaves Sunday afternoon and arrives in Bangkok on Tuesday, a journey of two nights. One way is currently $1,400 per person, double occupancy; round-trip gets you a 10-percent discount.

For information on both trains, call (800) 524-2420.

For Further Information

If you yearn for the days when train travel was the transportation of choice, get a free copy of "Railways to Adventure" from Maupintour, (800) 255-4266, (913) 843-1211. This company has assembled a number of vacations on restored and modern trains

If you take the leg from Dusseldorf, which stops in Cologne and Frankfurt before ending in Venice, you'll save: One way costs $1,600, round-trip, $2,320.

throughout Europe, Britain, Mexico, the United States, and Canada.

For information on the *Orient Express* and other refurbished train trips in Britain, Europe, and the United States, contact Abercrombie & Kent, 1520 Kensington Road, Oak Brook, IL 60521; (800) 323–7308 or (630) 954–2944.

A POTPOURRI OF TRAIN GOODIES

Here's a sampling of ways you can enjoy train travel.

- *GREAT BRITAIN.* An economical way to tour both Ireland and Britain is with a BritIreland pass, whereby you'll get unlimited train travel in the Republic of Ireland, Scotland, Wales, and Northern Ireland *plus* a round-trip cruise-style ferry crossing of the Irish Sea. The 30-day pass, recently priced at $445 for second class and $585 for first class, is good for five days of travel. A one-month pass provides ten days of travel for $625 for second class and $855 for first class.

  $ TIP If you're over age sixty, ask for a senior discount (you must prepurchase the pass in the United States).

  There are also passes for Scotland only. They include ferries to the Hebridean Islands and some local buses as well as a pass for Britain and France and for England and Wales.

  For information contact BritRail Travel International, 1500 Broadway, New York, NY 10036; (800) 677–8585 or (212) 575–2667 in New York. Ask for these free publications: *British Rail Pocket Timetable, Scenic Rail Journeys,* and *Go BritRail.*

- *THE CHUNNEL.* Rail Europe's new high-speed Eurostar service through the Chunnel links Paris to London in three hours, and Brussels to London in three hours fifteen minutes. Lowest fare, "Discovery Special," a fourteen-day second-class advance purchase, is $75, nonrefundable and nonexchangeable. Bernard Frelat, president of Rail Europe Group, told us that "this compares favorably with the best current London–Paris airfare, which runs above $100." If you don't want to risk the nonrefundable advance purchase ticket, regular Paris/London tickets in second class are $170 and $241 in first class. First class includes a breakfast, lunch, or dinner served at your seat, free newspapers, and access to a special lounge in London's Waterloo Station. Service through the Channel Tunnel takes about twenty minutes with trains traveling at 100 miles per hour. There are frequent departures and reservations are compulsory. Obtain tickets from Rail Europe, (800) EUROSTAR, or from BritRail Travel, (800) 677-8585 or (212) 575-2667 in New York.

- *IRELAND.* Get unlimited bus *or* train travel at reduced rates by using the Rambler Pass throughout Ireland, priced at $108 for eight days or $162 for fifteen days. A "combination pass" lets you use both trains and buses and costs $150 for eight days or $207 for twelve days. The eight-day passes are good for a fifteen-day period, whereas the 12-day tickets are valid for thirty days.

   $ TIP Children under sixteen pay 50 percent less. For information call CIE Tours at (800) CIE-TOUR.

- *RUSSIA.* The relatively new Russian Flexipass gives unlimited train travel for any four days during a fifteen-day period, and extra days can be purchased. The Flexipass, valid on trains between all major cities, such as Moscow, St. Petersburg, and Kiev, was recently priced at $289 per person for first class and $198 for second class. Call Rail Europe at (800) TGV-RAIL; (800) 361-RAIL in Canada.

- *GRAND CANYON RAILWAY.* For detailed information call (800) 843-8724.

- *RAIL CANADA.* This government-owned passenger railroad can be reached by calling (800) 561-3949.

Where to Buy Rail Passes

Although most rail passes can be purchased in Europe, the Eurailpass generally cannot. For passes and more information, contact the following:

- BritRail Travel International, 1500 Broadway, New York, NY 10036; (212) 575-2667. *Handles:* BritFrance, BritGermany, BritIreland, BritRail, Chunnel tickets.

- CIE Tours International, 100 Hanover Avenue, Cedar Knolls, NJ 07927; (800) 243-8687 or (201) 292-3899. *Handles:* Britain, Ireland.
- CIT Rail, 342 Madison Avenue, Suite 207, New York, NY 10173; (800) 223-7987 or (212) 697-2100. *Handles:* Eurail, Germany, Italy.
- DER Tours/German Rail, 9501 West Devon Avenue, Suite 400, Rosemont, IL 60018; (800) 421-2929. *Handles:* Eurail, Benelux, Austria, Britain, Germany, Italy.
- Forsyth Travel Library, Box 480800, Kansas City, MO 64148. *Handles:* numerous rail passes, including Central Europe, plus timetables and travel books.
- Netherlands Board of Tourism, 225 North Michigan Avenue, Chicago, IL 60601; (312) 819-0300. *Handles:* Benelux, Netherlands.
- Orbis Polish Travel Bureau, 342 Madison Avenue, New York, NY 10173; (800) 223-6037 or (212) 867-5011. *Handles:* European East, Austria, Czech Republic, Hungary, Poland.
- Rail Europe, 226 Westchester Avenue, White Plains, NY 10604; (800) 438-7245. *Handles:* Eurail, Benelux, BritFrance, European East, Scandinavia, Czech Republic, France, Greece, Hungary, Poland, Portugal, Russia, Spain, Switzerland, and Euro Star.
- Scandinavian American World Tours, 933 Highway 23, Pompton Plains, NJ 07444; (800) 545-2204 or (201) 835-7070. *Handles:* Eurail, Scandinavia.
- Scantours, 3439 Wade Street, Los Angeles, CA 90066; (800) 223-7226. *Handles:* Eurail, Scandinavia, Finland.

Books on Train Travel in Europe

- *Europe by Eurail* by George and LaVerne Ferguson, Globe Pequot, updated annually; $14.95.
- *Eurail Guide* by Kathryn M. Turpin and Marvin L. Saltzman, Eurail Guide Annual; $14.95.
- *Europe by Train* by Katie Wood and George McDonald, Harper Perennial; $14.00.

LEAVE THE DRIVING TO US: BUS TRAVEL

There's nothing mysterious about bus travel in the United States. Bear in mind, nevertheless, that long trips can wind up being as expensive (or almost) as train or plane travel if you pay for your meals and/or hotel or motel rooms. On short routes, however, the bus is very economical, and since travel is from center city to center city, very convenient as well.

To figure out whether you should take the train, plane, or bus, fill in the worksheet on the next page.

Greyhound from time to time has advance-purchase, rock-bottom rates. (See the table below for sample rates.)

For a free copy of *The Motorcoach Travel Directory,* which lists 700 members and type of service, arranged by state, call American Bus Association, (800) 283–2877.

Sample Advance-Purchase Rates on Greyhound Bus

Route	Standard	7-Day Advance	14-Day Advance	21-Day Advance
New York City–Dallas	$290.00	$232.00	$188.50	$134.00
Los Angeles–San Francisco	84.00	67.20	54.60	42.00
Los Angeles–Phoenix	51.00	48.80	33.15	25.50
New York City–Boston	42.00	–	20.80	16.00
New York City–Washington	25.00	–	–	–

Train, Plane, or Bus?

Route:_____

	Train	Plane	Bus
Regular fare	$_____	$_____	$_____
Advanced fare	$_____	$_____	$_____
Excursion/night fare	$_____	$_____	$_____
Senior discount fare	$_____	$_____	$_____
Weekend discount fare	$_____	$_____	$_____
Taxi/bus to/from station or airport	$_____	$_____	$_____
Meals	$_____	$_____	$_____
Hotel/motel room (may be included with package)	$_____	$_____	$_____
Totals:	$_____	$_____	$_____

Bus Travel in Europe

The EuropaBus, an extensive network of motor-coach routes, operates in conjunction with each country's railroad system. Travel is generally less pricey than by train. For information on fares and how to purchase passes, contact EuropaRail, DER Tours, Inc., 1933 Wilshire Boulevard, Los Angeles, CA 90025; (800) 937-1234 or (310) 479-4411.

$ TIP Whether in the United States or abroad, always ask about discounts for seniors, children, and families. Excursion, weekend, and special promotional rates will also cut your cost.

4

BEHIND THE WHEEL: TRAVELING BY CAR

The automobile—a walking stick; and one of the finest things in life is going on a journey with it.

— *Robert Holliday*

IT'S TRUE; driving a car—your own or a rented one—certainly comes with a lot of advantages, especially for trips that aren't too long. It's convenient, you can take along as much baggage as you want, and you can go exactly where you want, door to door.

It seems terribly logical, doesn't it? After all, your car is there, parked in front of your house or in the garage, so why not use it? You should, especially for short trips, but before pulling out of the driveway for a longer journey, think twice. Will you be bored? Are there too many of you crammed into the back seat? Can your back take it? Are the kids likely to get car sick? Will you push to cover too many miles in too short a time? Before packing the overhead rack with your tent, canoe, and bikes, read chapter 7, Traveling with Children, on how to make family travel a happy occasion.

If, on the other hand, you decide to drive, take time to do all those obvious yet important things your dad told you about that help prevent disasters. One of the perpetual pretrip nightmares vacationers have is that the car will break down on the road in the middle of a storm or heat wave, with the whole family fussing and fuming as hundreds of stalled motorists behind you honk loudly. To prevent this nightmare from turning into stark reality, do the following.

- Get a tune-up.
- Check the level of all fluids: gas, oil, coolant, windshield cleaner.
- Test the air pressure in the tires.
- Find the spare tire.
- Replace the windshield wipers.
- Locate your license and car registration.
- Know where you're going and mark the route on a map.
- Put your auto club materials in the glove compartment, along with the map.

HOW THE AUTOMOBILE CLUBS STACK UP

If after taking all these precautions, trouble comes honking, you'll be glad you joined an auto club. The average car on the road is now almost seven and a half years old, so it makes good sense to belong to a club. There are seventeen national clubs around the country competing with the oldest—the 36-million-member American Automobile Association (AAA). For an annual fee they all offer similar roadside services: fixing flats, delivering gasoline, jump-starting engines, towing your vehicle. In some cases for an extra few dollars you get additional goodies, such as extra trip-interruption insurance. Some clubs provide 10- to 50-percent discounts on hotel rooms and other travel expenses.

According to a recent survey of the eight largest clubs, the Exxon Travel Club was found to be the best deal for most drivers, simply because it has the greatest number of contracted emergency-service providers as well as family coverage. Second place went to AAA. Here's what you need to consider:

1. *If you have an older car,* pick a club that has excellent road service for free. (A *Money* magazine survey warns against Chevron, which has no contracted service providers.)
2. *If you have lots of drivers in your family,* pick a club that covers all of them. (Most clubs simply cover spouses and charge $12 to $20 more per year for each extra person.) Exxon's basic membership covers spouses, children up to age nineteen, and unmarried domestic partners.
3. *If you take long vacations by car,* pick a club with good trip-routing service. Allstate and AAA are particularly good.
4. *If you tend to lose your keys or lock yourself out of your car,* pick a club with a good lock-out plan, such as Amoco, Exxon, or Cross Country.
5. *If you're looking for discounts,* AAA gives 10 to 40 percent off at 45,000 retail establishments throughout the country. AAA and Exxon give up to 50 percent off at major hotel chains.
6. *If you drive abroad,* sign up with AAA. It is the only club that provides contracted free road service in most countries.
7. *If you have a luxury car,* you may automatically be enrolled in the Cross Country Motor Club.

To determine which club is best for you, call each for answers to these questions:

- Will I be towed? How far? How much will it cost?
- What if my spouse has trouble in another car?
- What if I don't have cash with me?
- What if I lock my keys in my car?
- What if I need road help while I'm driving a friend's car?
- What travel insurance comes with my membership?
- Is there trip continuation money if I have an accident away from home?
- Do you pay for ambulance service?
- Do you have credit-card protection?
- Do you plan trips? Provide maps?
- Do you give senior citizens a discount?
- Do you have cellular-phone service?
- Do you cover vans, trucks, antique cars, luxury models?

Two phrases you will encounter as you shop the clubs are these: *trip continuation allowance,* which reimburses you for lodging, meals, and other expenses incurred after an accident; and *lockout plan,* which pays for a locksmith to get into your car and possibly into your home if you've lost your house or apartment keys as well.

To compare the advantages of various automobile clubs, fill out the worksheet on the following page.

RENTING A CAR: HOW TO AVOID THE POTHOLES

The world of car renting has become increasingly complex; simply having a valid driver's license and a credit card is no longer enough. Today there are a myriad of rental companies, rules, regulations, and deals. Chances are you're like most people and won't take the time to read all the fine print in the rental contract before you pull out of the lot, so here are the questions you should ask and the facts you should know about car rentals.

Some research and advance planning will increase your chances of renting the car you want at the best possible price.

Before You Get to the Counter

- *How's your driving record?* Many rental firms can now look at your driving record by tapping into computerized data supplied by state departments of motor vehicles. You will be rejected if the company considers you a bad risk. What's a bad risk? If you have a drunk-driving conviction or several moving violations within the past twenty-four to forty-eight months. Self-defense: Call the company first and ask about their policy. Turn to the smaller companies, which have not yet begun to check.
- *Special equipment needs.* Many companies need at least twenty-four hours advance notice if you want a station wagon, luggage rack, child's seat, smoke-free car, or one designed for the disabled.
- *Shop around.* A phone call or two will pay off. For example, summer 1997 rates in the Orlando International Airport for

WORKSHEET

Comparing the Auto Clubs

CLUB/PHONE	ANNUAL FEE	YOUR NOTES
AAA local office or (800) 222–4357	$45.00 average, but varies within 130 individual clubs	_____
Allstate (800) 255–2582	$54.95	_____
Amoco Motor Club (800) 334–3300	$59.95	_____
Chevron (800) 255–2273	$39.00	_____
Exxon (800) 833–9966	$66.00	_____
Montgomery Ward (800) 621–5151	$62.00	_____
Road America (800) 262–7262	$59.00	_____
Shell Motorist Club (800) 621–8663	Varies; $45.00 to $54.00	_____

one week for a mid-sized sedan ranged from $150 with
Thrifty to $245 for Avis and Hertz.

- *Tally up the extras.* Many airports and cities have extra fees and
  taxes. Surcharges for additional drivers and special equipment are also common. If you're under age twenty-five, the
  big companies won't rent to you, but Alamo and Thrifty
  will—for $10 to $20 extra a day.

Collision Damage Waiver

Within the rental world collision-damage waiver is the most common area of confusion, full of changing regulations and misin-
formation. CDW, as it is called, pays for damage you do to the
rental car, and this premium can run anywhere from $4.50 to
$16.00 per day, depending on the amount of coverage. New York
and Illinois do not permit CDW sales, and California, Indiana,
Nevada, and Texas have dollar limits on CDW charges.

You may not need to pay for the additional collision-
damage insurance offered by the rental company if you already
have coverage through your personal automobile insurance or
your credit-card company. Check both in advance of renting.
(Most U.S. automobile-insurance policies do not apply when
you're driving outside the United States or Canada; some credit-
card coverage does. Among the things you need to check on are
these:

- Does my personal automobile insurance policy limit the
  amount of damage it will pay to the value of my personal
  car? If so, and if you rent a more valuable car than your own,
  you'll need additional coverage.
- Does my credit-card or personal insurance collision-damage
  insurance cover additional drivers listed on the rental contract?
- How long is my rental insurance good for? American
  Express covers thirty-one days; MasterCard and Visa, fifteen
  days.
- Does my insurance cover unusual cars (such as a Mercedes),
  minivans, trailers, recreational vehicles, campers, and
  trucks? What about antique and exotic cars?

- Does my insurance cover damage to the other car?
- What is my deductible? (If you have a $500 deductible for collision damage to your personal car, then you will be responsible for the first $500 damage to a rental car. *Note:* Your credit card may pick up your deductible.)
- What personal-effect coverage do I have?
- What coverage do I have for personal injury? Car companies offer an umbrella liability policy for up to $1 million of coverage. It costs $8.00 to $9.00 per day but is unnecessary if you already have personal-liability coverage with your own auto insurance or if you carry a separate liability policy.

   CAUTION ☞ If you are in an accident caused because you were under the influence of drugs or alcohol, most credit-card collision-damage policies will not pay any claims.

Another point to keep in mind: When signing the rental agreement, put in the name of every additional family member driver, unless the form reads that "immediate family members may drive the car." If not, any collision-damage or liability insurance will be null and void in the event of an accident caused by a driver not listed on the form.

If the Car Breaks Down

You'll find that generally the larger rental car companies are more helpful than the smaller ones if your car breaks down. Regardless of who rented you the car, however, you're not financially responsible. Most rental companies pay for towing and mechanical repairs. An exception: breakdown due to off-the-road or illegal use of the car.

Before leaving the car-rental office, always ask for the phone number to call in case of trouble. Also jot down the license number and color of the car so that you can find it in a big parking lot or report it if it's stolen.

If you do break down, check the agreement (given to you when you rented the car or in the glove compartment) and follow the directions. In all cases notify the rental agency as soon as possible. Never make repairs until you've received authorization from the company. Self-defense: If you're in a remote spot or foreign country and you simply must make repairs, keep all receipts for reimbursement.

Paying for Gas

Rental companies continually change the rules on who pays for the gas. Ask if it is to your advantage to return the car with a full tank of gas.

SMART TIPS FOR CAR RENTERS

Here are sixteen smart tips to keep in mind when you rent a car.

1. *Don't rent* if you're simply going to go to one place, such as a hotel. Instead take the hotel shuttle, a cab, a limo, or public transportation.
2. *Start with your travel agent.* Your travel agent can scan computerized reservation systems for low rental prices and short-term deals. Some larger firms give travel agents discount coupons good for up to 20 percent off at hotels, free car upgrades, and, occasionally, 10 percent off rental rates. Ask your agent, too, about fly-drive packages.
3. *Reserve small.* Rental companies tend to have more large-sized models on hand than smaller ones. That means there's a good chance that if you reserve a compact at the cheaper rate, it will not be available when you arrive. Then you'll be upgraded to a larger car at no extra cost.
4. *Ask the rental company for the car with the least mileage.* This information is in their computer but rarely volunteered.
5. *Don't rent a car at the airport.* "Off-airport" car-rental companies don't have to pay airport taxes and high fees for being on the site, so they charge you less. Doing this, however, requires patience, as they're often difficult to find. Self-defense: Take the shuttle or bus to your hotel; check the yellow pages for alternative car-rental firms.
6. *Look for the little guys.* The feisty companies, such as Alamo, Thrifty, National, Agency, Enterprise, and Snappy, are often 10 to 20 percent cheaper than Hertz, Avis, and National. There are also companies not affiliated with the

chains that may have even lower rates: in Los Angeles and San Francisco, call Bob Leech Autorental at (800) 364–3271; in Chicago and Indianapolis call Ace Rent a Car at (800) 323–3221; in Houston, Austin, and San Antonio call Montgomery Ward at (800) 524–8136; and in the Sunbelt states, call Value Rent-A-Car at (800) 327–6459.

7. *Skip beauty.* You'll pay less for cars from Rent-a-Wreck (800–535–1391), Ugly Duckling (800–843–3825), and U Save (800–272–8728). Be prepared for a car that's older and has some dents or scratches but is in good mechanical condition.

8. *Use the right credit card.* Use a credit card that has a high or an unlimited credit line, such as American Express. Some rental companies put a hold of up to $2,500 on cards while you're driving their car around. Check the fine print in the contract where such restrictions are spelled out. This can put you at or over your limit, making it difficult or impossible to charge meals, hotel rooms, or purchases.

9. *Quote rates.* If you read about a low rate in the newspaper, move quickly, as these are often short-lived. When reserving, mention the ad and the discount code, which is listed in small print beneath the rate, or in the description of the terms and conditions of rental. Better yet, bring a copy of the ad with you to the rental counter.

10. *Drop names.* Always mention clubs or associations to which you belong, such as a professional trade or travel group, including Amoco Motor Club, AAA, AARP, American Small Business Association, American Bar Association, National Association of Retired Federal Employees, National Association for the Self-Employed, or any travel club, as well as the name of your employer or corporation. You may be entitled to at least a 10-percent discount. (Also keep the association or club's toll-free number with you in case you need assistance.)

11. *Check out the car before driving away.* You are not obligated to take the car you're given if, for some reason, it doesn't suit you. Have major dents and scratches noted on your contract, and make certain there is a spare tire, jack, and window scraper.

12. *Join a frequent-renter program if you rent often.* Hertz #1 Gold, Budget Frequent-Renter Reward Plan, or National's Emerald Aisle offer upgrades, quicker check-in and check-out, and sometimes discounts.

13. *Understand your insurance.* Don't fall for the rental firm's hard-sell tactics about collision-damage waivers that relieve you from financial responsibility if you damage the car. In most cases your personal insurance or your credit card will automatically cover collision damage, so avoid being sucked into buying the $7–$15/day CDW. Each time you rent a car check with your insurance company and your credit-card issuer, as they may have withdrawn this protection without your knowledge since the last time.

    CAUTION ☛ Credit card companies provide only collision coverage, not liability coverage.

14. *Plan the hour.* If you're renting at or near the airport, book flight arrival and departure times for the same time of day to avoid hourly overtime charges that, if you're not careful, can mount up and be as high as the daily rate.

15. *Avoid late-return penalties.* Ask the car-rental company exactly what time you *must* return the car. Some companies give at least a one-hour grace period and then charge an hourly late-return rate. Some companies charge an additional half or full day for being just one hour over the deadline.

16. *Know the one-way drop-off fee.* If you return the car to a city other than the one you rented it in, know the price for doing so. It can be hefty.

PROTECT YOURSELF AND THE CAR FROM TOURIST CRIME

Unfortunately, we've all been forced to come to grips with the surge in auto thefts, highway crimes, and tourist attacks in and around our nation's cities and even in some rural areas. Those driving out-of-state and rental cars are natural victims because they are apt to be carrying more luggage and valuables than the natives. *Self defense:* Make your car look as much like a resident's as possible, and use common sense:

- *Don't accept a car that has markings designating it as a rented car,* such as the name of the rental company on a sticker on the license plate.
- *Ask for specific directions to your destination* before you leave the rental counter. If you do become lost, do not pull over on the side of the road to study your map. Instead, find a well-lighted, populated public place, such as a service station.
- *Don't park an obvious rental car in an unprotected lot* or on a dark street. Thieves target these cars for luggage and cameras.
- *Keep luggage and valuables in the trunk* and lock it.
- *Place your purse, wallet, briefcase, tote bag, and maps on the floor,* and not on the front passenger seat.
- *Never ask directions from strangers.*
- *Never stop if a driver flashes his headlights at you.* Instead, drive to the first well-lighted and busy gas station or a police station.
- *Don't pick up hitchhikers.*

Amazing Annual Car Rental Deal:

Every year car rental agencies must move part of their fleets to the south or to ski areas during winter to meet seasonal demand. Look for ads in the newspaper. Our picks:

- Avis and Preferred Holidays' "See America" program. For around $300, you get a rental car, hotel vouchers for a week, plus one-way fare. You must pick up the car in Florida or Arizona and then drive to the Northeast or California, or vice versa. Your airfare home will be paid by Avis. For information call (800) 990-1919. (Preferred Holidays is Avis' tour subsidiary. Call 800-508-5454.)
- National Car Rental has a similar deal. Call (800) CAR-RENT and ask for rate code FLDR.

- *Don't stop to inspect damage* if you are bumped in the rear on a lonely road or even on a major highway. Instead, drive to the nearest police station or simply forget it.
- *Don't stop for a car with flashing red or yellow lights* unless you're certain it's a police car.
- *Don't drive home if you think you're being followed.* Instead, make a series of left turns. If after four such turns the vehicle in question is still following you, drive immediately to the nearest police station or busy gas station.
- *Keep windows and doors locked* when stopping at a red light or stop sign. Carjackers and others up to no good often prey on legitimately stopped cars.

THE NEW CELLULAR-PHONE SERVICES

A good way to protect yourself on the highway is to have a car cellular service. In fact, it may already be part of your telephone package. If not, it easily can be added for a nominal monthly fee.

The cellular-phone companies' emergency roadside assistance programs will send a locksmith, bring gas, jump-start dead batteries, change flats, and tow disabled cars—all for a monthly fee that ranges from zero for some customers to $3.95 at US West Cellular.

A similar service comes with most new-car warranties. Starting with the 1994 models, almost all auto manufacturers began following the lead of luxury-car makers by offering roadside assistance as part of their basic warranty. With this service you simply dial a special number and within minutes a tow truck rescues you. Exceptions as of press time are Chrysler, Toyota, and Honda.

Rescue service is also provided by the automobile clubs, discussed on page 73. For example, AAA sells cellular telephones with a "safety button" that automatically connects you to AAA Emergency Road Service. For information call (800) 222-4357.

A POTPOURRI OF SMART DRIVING TIPS

1. *Pump your own gas.* You'll save about 14 cents per gallon on all octane levels. If you're disabled, you still get the discount, although the attendant does the pumping.
2. *Drive under the speed limit.* You'll conserve gas and avoid expensive speeding tickets.
3. *Don't overload the carrier* on the top of the car. It can lower your gas mileage and be hazardous in a high wind.
4. *Carry a picnic basket, an ice chest, or a thermos* to cut food costs.
5. *Use a reliable gas station.* Premium gas isn't always premium. AAA estimates that as much as half the time, octane is lower than claimed on premium pumps. Very few states conduct gasoline quality tests on a regular basis and, as of press time, six states had no standards for gasoline quality: Kentucky, Ohio, Oregon, Pennsylvania, West Virginia, and Wyoming.
6. *Remember:* The majority of accidents take place in good weather when people are not exercising the same degree of caution as they do during fog, rain, snow, or storms.

DRIVING AND RENTING ABROAD

You'll find that driving in a foreign country is not quite the same as it is at home, but then, that's why you're going there—to experience something different. For example, air conditioning and automatic transmissions are not standard in European rental cars

---

Travel Trivia

Enlightened Auto Travel: A study by Avis discovered that motorists who drive with headlights on during the day have fewer severe accidents than those with no lights on. Damage severity in the nonlight group was 69 percent greater than in the group with cars with lights on.

The Leading Car-Rental Firms

Alamo	(800) 522-9696
Auto Europe	(800) 223-5555
Avis	(800) 331-1084
Budget	(800) 472-3325
DER Tours	(800) 782-2424
Eurodollar	(800) 800-6000
(Dollar Rent-a-Car in the United States)	
Europcar	(800) 227-3876
(National in the United States)	
European Car	(800) 535-3303
Europe by Car	(800) 223-1516
Eurorent	(800) 521-2235
Hertz	(800) 654-3001
ITS	(800) 521-0643
Kemwel/Holiday	(800) 678-0678
Payless	(800) 237-2804
Thrifty	(800) 331-9111

except on expensive luxury models. You can get them but they cost extra. Gasoline is much more expensive, often $5.00 a gallon.

Most European countries recognize a U.S. driver's license, but in Greece, Hungary, Russia, and Spain you'll need an International Driving Permit, which is valid for one year. Start the paperwork about a month in advance by calling your local AAA office or (800) AAA-HELP for the necessary forms. You'll need your license, two passport-type photographs, and $10.

Note: As we go to press, you cannot drive a rental car in China, Egypt, or Nepal; they come with chauffeurs.

Here's what you need to know.

- *Rent in the United States.* You'll save up to 50 percent over renting in a foreign country. You might save even more if you prepay here in dollars. You can rent foreign cars from U.S. rental companies—such as Alamo, Avis, Budget, Hertz,

Payless, Kemwel, and Thrifty—as well as from tour opera-
tors—such as Auto Europe, Europe by Car, DER Tours,
European Car Reservations, Eurorent, Foremost, Holiday
Autos, and ITS.

- Ask about the following, regardless whom you rent from: air
  conditioning, shift or automatic, size, payment up front or
  at end, return fees, VAT rate, country-to-country, driver age
  requirement, U.S. or international driver's license
- *Let the agent know* how many people there will be as well as
  how much luggage. Some European models are very small,
  especially by American standards.
- *Know if you're insured.* Your auto insurance and credit-card
  coverage may not extend overseas.

$ TIP Our favorites for low rates: Kemwel and Auto Europe.
Auto Europe, with more than 4,000 locations throughout
Europe, guarantees the best rates; in fact, if you find a lower one,
the company will beat it. It has car-rental counters inside airport
terminals, but hotel delivery is also available. There's no cancellation charge, and rates are guaranteed in dollars. The company is
also in the hotel business and has many excellent discounts.

OVERSEAS MOTOR-HOME TOURS

If you want to see the world in an RV, contact Overseas
Motorhome Tours in Redondo Beach, California, at (800)
322-2127. They have organized tours in Europe, with reasonably
priced round-trip airfare from the East Coast. Most are planned
so that you do your own driving and simply wind up at the same
place with others by evening. The company will also design and
conduct tours for groups of twenty-four or more people.

Recently, a one-month trip with round-trip airfare from East
Coast cities, with everything included, was $5,000.

For more information about taking an RV vacation in Europe,
pick up a copy of *Exploring Europe by RV* (Globe Pequot Press,
$14.95; to order call 800-243-0495).

DRIVING SOMEONE ELSE'S CAR

Driving another person's car is definitely a cheap way to see the country, but first you have to find someone who needs to have his or her car driven from point A to point B. Of course this person could have the car transported by truck or train, but that's expensive. The inexpensive alternative is *you*.

There are three basic systems. The first, known as the *direct* method, involves placing a classified ad in a newspaper under the heading "Driver Available," offering to drive to, say, the West Coast or to Memphis; or alternatively, reading the ads run by those who are looking for a driver, which are usually found under the heading "Car Transport" or "Auto Transport." The two of you then make the deal directly. Usually no money changes hands. You pay for the gas, and the two of you will determine who pays for repairs and tolls. Have your agreement in writing.

Another variation on this theme is called *exchange transportation*. This occurs when the owner of the car goes with you to share expenses and driving. You can find out about exchange deals by reading notices on office, school, and college bulletin boards and by checking the classified ads in the newspapers.

Buying a Car Abroad

You can save about 10 percent off the cost of a Volvo, BMW, Mercedes, or Saab if you purchase the car in Europe and have it shipped back to the United States. You must make arrangements, however, with a U.S. dealer at least one month, preferably two, in advance, to make sure that you get the model you want. The car must be built to meet U.S. safety standards and pass all U.S. environmental tests prior to shipment.

$ TIP Save even more by purchasing the car at the very beginning of your vacation and pocketing what you would have shelled out for a rental vehicle.

The third method, *drive-away*, is somewhat more complicated and is run by agencies that transport cars for owners. These agencies are listed in the yellow pages under "Automobile Transport," or "Drive-Away Companies." Contact the agency, tell them where and when you'd like to go, and they'll let you know if they have a car going your way. You must have a valid license, several other forms of identification, and references. You will be required to leave a deposit, which will be returned at the end of the trip. You pay for your own gas and lodging, and while you can route your own trip, you cannot exceed a certain odometer mileage for the given distance.

Getting Someone Else to Drive Your Car

The Auto Driveaway Company, headquartered in Chicago, will drive your car from your home or business to your next out-of-town destination. Great if you're moving, or if you want your car on a long vacation. The company uses only professional drivers and/or very experienced, prescreened members of the public. Drivers pay for their own gas, tolls, motels, food.

Auto Driveaway has eighty offices in the United States and Canada. Check your phone book for the one nearest you or call (800) 346–2277.

5

CRUISES: LUXURY YOU CAN AFFORD

The sea: a highway between the doorways of the nations.

— Francis K. Lane

YOU SHOULD NOT miss the opportunity to sail upon this highway. In fact, for many of us, taking a cruise is a lifelong dream. It's also a smart dream, for cruising is an incredibly easy way to vacation. You can visit different ports of call, have a carefree few days or weeks at sea, alone or with family and friends, and, best of all, you unpack just once!

Cruise lines have innovative itineraries and creative on-board programs tailored to families, lovers, gourmands, sports enthusiasts, naturalists, historians, gamblers, and party people. On some ships kids can go to day camp, babies to the nursery, parents to lectures, and everyone to the pool.

Some 160 cruise ships are waiting for you to climb the gangplank. They range in size from several thousand passengers down to small sailing yachts, barges, and houseboats. You can ply the Mississippi River, the Caribbean, or the Baltic Sea. You can sign up for a three-day escape, a five-day crossing of the Atlantic, or a three-month 'round-the-world voyage.

Whichever or whatever you decide on, your ticket includes your cabin, all meals, entertainment, and activities. The ship lines are anxious to have you on board, and they offer all kinds of amenities to get you there: discounts, free airfare to and from the points of departure and return, upgrades to a better cabin, free precruise or postcruise hotel rooms, tours, and even credits you can use on board. After all, their costs are just about the same whether you go or not.

Nevertheless, beware. There are extra expenses, such as tips, shore excursions, and alcoholic drinks. (Check the fill-in worksheet on page 93.)

BEING A HAPPY SAILOR

To make certain that your cruise matches your dream, follow this strategy: Do some up-front homework and be clear about your personal preferences. If you need plenty of space around you or if you plan to spend time in your cabin, you must pick a cabin that is large enough. Many cabins are not; in fact, many are barely large enough to turn around in, let alone accommodate two people and all their luggage.

On the other hand, if you plan to spend most of your time on the deck, in the pool, or working out in the fitness center, you can save money by booking a smaller cabin.

If you're prone to seasickness, pick a large ship with good stabilization and a cabin in the middle-deck area. By all means avoid small ships designed for shallower waters and routes that cross open, choppy seas. Always ask your travel agent or the cruise line about this. Even whale-watching off the coast of California can be rough. Pick instead calmer waters: most of the Caribbean, the protected archipelagos in the South Pacific, Alaska's Inland Passage, the Pacific Coast, and, in the United States, voyages on the Columbia, Snake, Sacramento, Hudson, and Mississippi Rivers.

USING A CRUISE SPECIALIST

Ships also vary widely in terms of amenities, service, and itineraries, as well as the age and the socioeconomic profile of the pas-

---

The Seven Top Cruise Specialists

Cruise lines almost always offer discounts if you buy early or at the last minute. Even so you should shop around to find the best prices. In addition to asking your own travel agent, consult with one or more of these specialists:

All Cruise Travel	(800) 227-8473
Cruise Pro	(800) 222-7447
Cruises, Inc.	(800) 854-0500
Cruise Line, Inc.	(800) 777-0707
Cruises of Distinction	(800) 634-3445
World Wide Cruises	(800) 882-9000
Cruiseworld	(800) 321-2784

---

sengers. If you read the brochure, you obviously can get a clear fix on the itinerary, the layout of the ship, a list of activities, and the size of the cabins, but the brochures never tell you about your fellow passengers. It's extremely difficult to ascertain the passenger profile, although quite obviously expensive cruises are paid for by people who can afford them. But is the cruise geared toward singles? Families? People from certain parts of the country? An international clientele? A party crowd? **$ TIP** A good rule of thumb: Longer, more expensive cruises tend to attract an older, more affluent crowd, whereas shorter, less pricey cruises appeal to younger people, singles, and families. But the best ways to find out are to work with a cruise specialist, who can guide you in the right direction, and to ask friends who have taken cruises (see sidebar above).

Another good reason to use a cruise specialist is that you'll save money. Because there is no regulation of rates, different travel agents may quote you different rates for the very same ship, cabin, and itinerary. An agent who specializes in cruises not only will have the best deals but will also be familiar with individual ships and their character. These agents can often get you added amenities, cabin upgrades, and other goodies because they have extra clout with the cruise lines.

DETERMINING YOUR TRUE COSTS

Understanding Your Expenses

Although cruises are promoted as all-inclusive, meaning that food, on-board activities, drinks (nonalcoholic and sometimes alcoholic), and your cabin are paid for, there are optional extras that you may want to include in your budget. You'll enjoy your trip much more if you plan for them in advance. To avoid unpleasant hidden surprises, estimate what you're likely to spend on your cruise by filling in the budget worksheet My Cruise Dollars (see next page) before purchasing your ticket and traveler's checks.

LANDING A BARGAIN

Armed with the right information, you can find discounts on a great many cruises. The simplest way to cut the price of your ticket is to book early (anywhere from sixty days to a year in advance), as most lines have some kind of early-bird discount. They would rather have your money in their account as soon as possible; early booking also assures them that you are cruising on their line. As a result, to get you to book well in advance, most lines are willing to give you a substantial discount. You need to ask, however, so call the line directly and also check with one of the cruise specialists listed on page 91.

Traveling during the off-peak season is another way to save. For example, in the Caribbean, rates are typically lowest during spring and summer; in Alaska, early spring and late fall.

To get a bargain on a cruise, look for a ship that's "repositioning," the industry term for when a ship goes from service in one area to service in another, say from the Caribbean to the Mediterranean. Call your travel agent or the specialists listed on page 91 to learn of repositioning.

My Cruise Dollars

EXPENSES BEFORE BOARDING

Price of ticket $ _____

Toiletries, miscellaneous $ _____

Cruise clothes $ _____

Pet care (dog to kennel, etc.) $ _____

New luggage $ _____

Books and games $ _____

Hotel overnight before/after the cruise $ _____

Transportation to/from ship $ _____

Other $ _____

Subtotal $ _____

EXPENSES AFTER BOARDING

Hairdresser/barber $ _____

Spa/fitness fees $ _____

Telephone calls and faxes $ _____

Laundry/dry cleaning $ _____

Gambling/bingo $ _____

Alcoholic drinks and wine $ _____

On-board shopping $ _____

Excess-baggage fee $ _____

Postage and postcards $ _____

Photos $ _____

Souvenirs $ _____

Shore excursions and purchases $ _____

Tips $ _____

Other $ _____

Subtotal $ _____

Total $ _____

If you're flexible about the departure date and cabin location, go for a deep, last-minute discount—anywhere from a month to a week before sailing.

Ways to Cut Costs

Here are ten surefire ways to cut the cost of a cruise:

1. *Be flexible about your dates.*
2. *Ask about a discount* for second person or children.
3. *Find out if there's free airfare* to the departure city. If so, ask what the fare is. You may be able to get a cheaper rate on your own, or use your frequent-flyer award to get to the pier. Then you can pocket the flight allowance.
4. *Get a price quote* from several cruise specialists (see page 91) and see if your travel agent can match the rate or better it.
5. *Tell about yourself.* Discounts are often given to newlyweds and couples celebrating big-number wedding anniversaries, as well as senior citizens.
6. *Look for new ships,* new routes, third- or fourth-person-in-cabin discounts, twofers, and rates for children and seniors.
7. *Book a fly/cruise or air/sea ticket.* These packages include much-reduced, or even free, airfare from most major North American cities. Sometimes the package includes a program with one-way free airfare when the ship starts its voyage in one port and ends up in another. Other times it includes free round-trip airfare to the point of embarkation and disembarkation. It typically includes transfers between airport and ship.
8. *Get free trip insurance,* if offered, to protect against sudden cancellation, lost luggage, or other problems. Most cruise lines sell such insurance at about $50 a ticket, but ask to have it included in the price.
9. *Travel in a group.* Put together a dozen friends or colleagues and ask for a group discount. Policies vary, depending on time of year and space availability. A group cruise is a great idea for family reunions.
10. *Upgrade.* Large ships have some leeway in offering upgrades. If you think you can qualify, pay for the lowest-

cost cabin. Nicer cabins and suites often go for the asking. You might be upgraded one or more levels. Upgrades typically go to business travelers, anniversary/wedding couples, seniors, frequent travelers, and members of travel clubs and organizations. Speak up.

Even the venerable old lady the *QE 2* has reduced fares. For example, it offers a standby fare on its six-day voyage across the Atlantic from New York City to Southampton, England. At various times, when bookings are slow, Cunard runs a special deal in which you can bring a companion on this crossing for the price of full fare. Fares include all meals plus one-way economy airfare on British Airways between London and a number of U.S. cities. Depending on the grade of cabin you book, a special fare for a one-way flight on the *Concorde* from London to New York or to Washington, D.C., is also part of the package.

Who Has the Best Discounts and Deals?

These major cruise lines, among many others, offer particularly good discounts and packages at various times during the year. Call directly, then check with a cruise specialist.

Cunard	(800) 221-4770
Holland America	(800) 426-0327
Norwegian Cruise Line	(800) 327-7030
Radisson Seven Seas	(800) 285-1835
Renaissance Cruises	(800) 525-5350
Royal Viking	(800) 634-8000
World Explorer	(800) 854-3835

Getting Free Passage

Cruise lines are always looking for talent to keep passengers happy. If you fit into any of the categories they are looking for, you might get free passage and, possibly, a fee. Ships need experts in teaching and lecturing in foreign languages, finance and investing, botany, archaeology, gardening, gambling, history, golf, tennis, and bridge. At times they also need doctors and nurses. If you're a celebrity singer, a storyteller, an entertainer, a dancer, or a movie or TV personality, you may find a free berth.

A new category that might get you free passage is that of older, presentable, unattached men who are good dancers and willing to do the tango with unaccompanied women on board. It helps if you also play bridge. (For more on this type of free passage, see pp. 160 and 178.)

Cruises that specialize in family vacations need counselors—people with experience in taking care of and entertaining children from nursery-school age up through the teen years.

To apply, call any of the cruise lines and ask for the personnel department.

SLEEPING AND EATING

Choosing a Cabin

After you've selected an itinerary and a ship, your next important decision is the choice of a cabin. Go over the deck plan in the brochure very carefully, ideally with a cruise agent who is familiar with the ship. Don't be dumb and pick a cabin next to the restaurant or disco. Decide, too, if you want an inside or outside cabin. An inside cabin has no porthole and is dark twenty-four hours a day, but it is significantly cheaper than an outside cabin, which has a porthole or, on some ships, sliding glass doors onto a minideck.

$ TIP Study the cabin diagram carefully, noting the size; compare the amount of square feet with, say, your bedroom at home, to have a realistic sense of the space you're buying.

> ## Travel Trivia
>
> **Skip the Eggs:** A study by the Centers for Disease Control & Prevention found that eggs, served in a "pooled" fashion in large serving dishes, and undercooked shellfish accounted for one-third of the diarrhea outbreaks aboard cruise ships.

Another viewpoint: Book the least expensive cabin on the best ship that you can afford, rather than the most expensive cabin on the least expensive ship. Why? On all ships except the *QE 2,* passengers have equal access to all the public facilities, and, if you don't spend much time in your cabin, except to sleep, why not?

Dining Arrangements

All your meals will be on board (except for shore excursions), so you certainly want to be happy with your dining situation. If you want to dine only with your spouse or friend, make certain that the ship actually has tables for two before booking passage. Some have none, others only a very few.

If you are traveling with friends, request a table for your group; otherwise you will find yourself seated with strangers.

You will also be given a choice of early or late seating and whether you want to dine in a smoking or nonsmoking area. Generally, older people opt for the early seating and night owls pick the late one.

Your agent will relay your dining preferences and any special dietary requests to the ship when you pay for your ticket. In most cases you receive your dining-room assignment with your ticket and other documents, or a card with your table number and seating time will be in your cabin.

Note: If you find you don't care for your dining companions, ask the maitre d' to reassign you as soon as possible. It's a good idea to give him a $10 tip as an incentive for juggling things around. Don't be shy about seeking a change—you don't want to be "stuck" at every meal with people who are not your type—and, you never know, your tablemates may wish to dine with someone else, too.

TAKING SHORE EXCURSIONS

Shore excursions are, of course, not mandatory, but if you go, be prepared to pay anywhere from $10 to $150 per person, depending on the activity. The fee covers the cost of getting you ashore if it's in a smaller vessel. It may also cover guided tours of local sites, lunch or tea and snacks, and overnight shore accommodations, including drinks and dinner. If there's no planned on-shore program, you might want to join several other passengers and share the cost of a taxi ride to town or a guided tour of the area (this may in fact save you money over the cost of the standard shore excursion bought on board).

CRUISING OFFBEAT

Got a hankering to do something unusual? Read on. You'll discover that offbeat cruises are frequently less expensive than the traditional Caribbean cruise and even if not, they're always fascinating.

Theme Cruises

If you think that the standard cruise itinerary will leave you bored, try a theme cruise. It will add to your life, be it knowledge about art, wine, gardening, music, theater, or investing. You may even improve a skill such as cooking, golf, baseball, dancing, or speaking a foreign language. (See the table below for a list of cruise lines

Leading Theme Cruise Lines

Cunard	(800) 221-4770
Royal Viking	(800) 634-8000
Royal Caribbean	(800) 327-6700
Clipper Cruises	(800) 325-0010
Delta Queen	(800) 543-1949
World Explorer	(800) 854-3835

that add purpose to pleasure; call and ask them what theme cruises they have coming up.)

Cruising without Leaving the United States

You don't have to fly to a faraway port to start your cruise, nor do you have to leave North America once you're on board. Here are some ways to keep your cruise simple:

- *THE GREAT LAKES.* During summer, the ninety-passenger *Mayan Prince* cruises the four Great Lakes as well as along the New England coast. Call American Canadian Caribbean Line at (800) 556-7450.
- *MORE GREAT LAKES.* Three ten-day cruises aboard the new 420-passenger *Columbus* sail between Montreal and Chicago on Lakes Erie, Huron, Ontario, Superior, and Michigan. All itineraries include historic sites and a stop at Mackinaw Island. Call Hapag-Lloyd, (519) 624-5513.
- *THE HUDSON RIVER.* The lovely yacht *Teal* cruises from New York City to Troy, stopping at famous historic landmarks along the way, including West Point and President Franklin Delano Roosevelt's Hyde Park. Sleep at The Beekman Arms, America's oldest inn, and at a peaceful monastery. There are six fall trips, each one week long. Call River Valley Tours at (800) 836-2128.
- *THE MISSISSIPPI RIVER.* The quintessential river cruise is on the paddle wheeler that goes from New Orleans to St. Paul. Today you can take the *Delta Queen,* an elegant ship (designated a National Historic Landmark), which does not have air conditioning, and the *Mississippi Queen,* which does. The food on both ships is quite good, the accommodations rather small and basic, and the entertainment not terribly sophisticated. Shore excursions to river towns, Civil War sites, and southern mansions cost extra but are excellent and really worth the price. The whole cruise takes twelve days, but you can take shorter segments. Call Delta Queen Steamboat Co. at (800) 543-1949.
- *FLORIDA'S WATERWAYS.* The seventy-two-passenger *New Shoreham II* departs from West Palm Beach, crosses Lake Okeechobee to Sanibel, Sarasota, Panama City, Biloxi, and,

lastly, New Orleans. It has similar cruises on the Mississippi and through the bayou as well as a cruise that leaves West Palm Beach and sails to Rhode Island on the Atlantic Intracoastal Waterway. For information call American Odyssey Voyages at (800) 556-7450 or (401) 247-0955.

- *ALASKA DRIVE/CRUISE PACKAGE.* If you'd like to drive your camper or RV up the 1,000-mile Alaska Highway but can't stand the thought of getting behind the wheel for the long trip back, here's a solution. This nine-day cruise along the Gulf of Alaska and through the Inside Passage includes transport for your RV. You check your vehicle in at Anchorage for shipment on an enclosed oceangoing ship to Tacoma, Washington, where you pick it up after your cruise. For information call Gray Line of Alaska at (800) 628-3843.
- *MORE ALASKA.* The Alaska Sightseeing Cruise West Company specializes in small-ship cruises that take you very close to sites on two dramatic rivers, the Columbia and the Snake, through Glacier Bay, and into other places where the big ships simply can't go. For information call (800) 426-7702.
- *PUGET SOUND.* The 59-foot M/V *Sacajawea* cruises Puget Sound on the Inside Passage of British Columbia. An informal atmosphere pervades, with family-style meals. You'll sail only during the day, so you won't miss any great scenery while sleeping.

    $ TIP If you book a group of six, you can get a 10-percent discount. For information call Catalyst Cruise Line at (206) 537-7678.

Leaving Home

After you've exhausted local cruises you may want to test foreign waters. Here are some of our favorites:

- *RIVER BARGING.* River-barging trips are extremely popular in Europe and the United Kingdom. Although most of them end in late autumn, this company has two centrally heated luxury hotel barges that cruise in the south of France until mid-December and in Scotland all year round. The price of a six-night trip is considerably less in off-peak times than in the peak summer season. For information call European Waterways, c/o Le Boat, Inc., at (800) 217–4447 or (201) 342–1838. Other leading river-barging/cruise operators are KD River Cruises (800–346–6525), and Kemwel (800–234–4000).

- *EXOTIC NATURE CRUISES.* Take an elegant small ship and sail into very remote areas of the Arctic, the Aleutian Islands, and the Russian Far East. If you prefer to stay closer to home, sign up for a cruise along either coast of the United States or through the U.S. Intracoastal Highway. Naturalists and lecturers are on board. For information call Clipper Cruises at (800) 325–0010.

  Similar first-rate nature-oriented cruises are run by Special Expeditions. For information call them at (800) 762–0003.

  TIP Avoid the five claustrophobic cabins on the lower deck of the *Sea Bird* and *Sea Lion;* their portholes are almost useless for viewing.

- *DELIVER THE MAIL.* Every day one of the Bergen Line's eleven coastal steamers leaves Bergen, on the southern coast of Norway, and heads north, through a series of dramatic fjords, for ports within the Arctic Circle, and back again—a round-trip of 1,250 miles. Each ship carries cargo, mail, and a handful of passengers. You can go part of the way or all the way, and in between you can take interesting, inexpensive shore excursions. For information call Bergen Line at (800) 323–7436.

- *CRUISE ON A YACHT.* With Moorings Preferred Yacht Holidays you can cruise the Caribbean or South Pacific without chartering the entire ship. Book just a stateroom with a private bath and get access to the rest of the yacht, including the dining area. For more information call (800) 437–7880.

Windjammer and Tall Ship Cruises

Windjammers are sailing ships with auxiliary power, and passengers are allowed to help with the sailing. Sometimes they're called tall ships, schooners, or sloops, but whatever name they go by, they are much loved by those who prefer to cruise by wind rather than by motor, who opt for the unfurling of the canvas

Eight Tall Ship Companies

Here are eight companies to contact for information. Do so six months in advance of your vacation, if possible.

- Ocean Voyages, Sausalito, CA; (415) 332-4681
- Barefoot Windjammer Cruises, Miami, FL; (800) 327-2601, (305) 672-6453
- Maine Windjammer Association, Rockport, ME; (800) 624-6380, (207) 374-5400
- The Cruise Company, Greenwich, CT; (800) 825-0826, (203) 852-0941
- Tall Ship Adventures, Aurora CO; (800) 662-0090, (303) 755-7983
- Star Clippers, Coral Gables, FL; (800) 442-0551; (305) 442-0550
- Windjammer Cruises, Honolulu, HI; (808) 537-1122
- Yankee Schooner Cruises, Camden, ME; (800) 255-4449, (207) 236-4449

sail over the purr (some say churn) of the engine. These ships are found around the globe but are primarily centered in the Caribbean and off the coast of Maine. For the most part these cruises are less expensive and more informal and they attract a lively, young crowd.

$ TIP Dirigo Cruises in Clinton, Connecticut (860-669-7068) represents a number of windjammer cruises that sail out of ports around the globe.

Before booking:

1. *Make certain you're not susceptible to seasickness*—after all, you won't be sailing on the stable *QE 2*. Or take along appropriate medication.
2. *Talk to someone* who has been on this type of sailing trip to get an idea of what to expect.

3. *Gather as much literature as you can;* it will help you make a decision about whether or not this is your cup of tea, what the ship is like, and where you'll be sailing.

4. *Call one of the cruise specialists* (see page 91) or your travel agent, if he or she is knowledgeable in this area, and ask what the accommodations are *really like.* You may have to share a cabin or a shower; space may be very tight. If you need privacy, make certain you can indeed have it . . . and at what price.

Freighter Travel

Sailing by tramp steamer, as freighters were once called, is somewhat less romantic than the term implies. Neither Humphrey Bogart nor Sydney Greenstreet will be on the voyage, nor is it any longer a really cheap means of transportation. On the other hand, freighter travel holds special appeal for those who love an adventure into the unknown and who are willing to forgo luxury and nightlife to accompany a cargo of bananas or diamonds bound for distant ports with exotic-sounding names.

Keep in mind that freighter lines are essentially in the freight business; transporting passengers is secondary. Their itineraries, although firm, are not engraved in stone. They can and do change their schedules, but you won't be charged more for extra days at sea. You simply need to be flexible in terms of time.

Be prepared: Cabins vary considerably, from small to outside full-facility singles and doubles, but none are in the four-star category. You may dine with officers or at separate tables for passengers only. The food will be plentiful but not gourmet quality. Entertainment is pretty much limited to reading, board and card games, videos, and sing-alongs, although some freighters have swimming pools and exercise equipment. An exception is Ivaran's *Americana,* which has gambling, a bar, and a pianist.

The number of passengers is usually twelve or fewer, because the presence of a physician is required on board when there are more than twelve passengers. Many have an upper age limit that varies from seventy-five to eighty-two.

Because freighters rarely advertise, you'll need to book through one of these two specialized agencies:

1. Freighter World Cruises, 180 South Lake Avenue, Pasadena, CA 91101; (818) 449-3106. This company acts as the exclusive passenger agent in North America for fourteen freighter lines.
2. TravLtips, Box 188, Flushing, NY 11358; (800) 872-8584, (718) 939-2400. This travel agency publishes a bimonthly listing of services, discounted trips, and general freighter travel information, $25/year. **$ TIP** The firm also handles unusual cruises as well as inexpensive repositioning voyages. Ask, too, for copies of their free pamphlets.

You can also get ideas from the standard reference book *Ford's Freighter Travel Guide and Waterways of the World,* at your library, or for $15.95 from Ford's Travel Guides, 19448 Londelius Street, Northridge, CA 91324; (818) 701-7414.

Note: If you're single, you might like to know that Ivaran Line's *Americana* is the first and, as far as we know, the only passenger freighter with gentlemen hosts on board. These unpaid, unattached men (age fifty and over) will dance with, play cards with, and escort women who are traveling alone on shore excursions. If you're interested in being a gentleman host on a cruise, call (800) 451-1639.

FAMILY CRUISING

Cruises are ideal for family reunions. They let everyone do what they like. Because you can all go your own way during the day, too much "togetherness" is not a problem, when you gather together for meals. Among the lines that specialize in family cruises are Premier, Regency, and Carnival.

For telephone numbers and more information about family cruises, see page 137 in chapter 7, Traveling with Children.

CRUISES FOR THE PHYSICALLY HANDICAPPED

Le Boat, Inc., operates vessels that provide facilities for people in wheelchairs and for other disabled travelers. You can go barging in France and yachting in the Caribbean. For more information call (800) 922-0291 or (201) 342-1838.

PICKING THE BEST INSURANCE

In view of the fact that you must pay in advance for your entire cruise, trip insurance is important. Should you have to cancel at the last minute, you could lose the whole amount if you don't have coverage. Cruise lines and travel agents usually sell insurance, or you can buy a policy on your own.

Before purchasing the cruise line's protection, study it carefully with your cruise specialist or insurance agent. Many are simply waivers and do not take care of all the likely reasons why you might not make the trip. Some, for example, cease coverage the minute you leave home, so if you become ill on the flight or the night before in the debarkation city, you'll get no money back. Others will not cover you if you cancel less than seventy-two hours before sailing. Find out, too, if there are any preexisting conditions that exclude coverage and which relatives are covered under "due to illness in the family" clause.

Two policies that have good track records are Cruise and Tour from Mutual of Omaha (800-228-9792) and Travel Guard from CNA (800-826-1300). The Mutual of Omaha policy, with $5,000 of trip-cancellation coverage, costs about $265 for one person. Travel Guard provides $5,000 in trip-cancellation coverage for $311.

TIPPING JUST RIGHT

Unless tipping is included in the price of your cruise (in which case it's called an all-inclusive cruise, and you'll be told), you are expected to tip all those who helped you during the voyage, with the exception of the ship's captain and its officers.

Traditional thinking is to tip everyone the last night on board. We disagree. You're much more likely to obtain good service if you tip as you go along (remember: the word *tip* stands for "to insure promptness").

Cruise lines have printed guidelines suggesting how much to tip. This information is usually left in your cabin. If not, request a copy from the purser's office. Do so on the first, not the last, day. Then make it a point to give a portion of the total amount recommended to each person as they initially help you: the maître d' the first evening, the cabin steward when he or she does something useful, and the wine steward and your waiter at the end of the first dinner. Depending on the length of the cruise, tip everyone yet again halfway through the voyage and on the final day.

The recommended amounts on most cruise lines are $3.50 a day each for your waiter and your cabin steward and $1.50 a day for the busboy. This is absolute minimum; if they are particularly good, be more generous. They depend heavily on tips. If you order wine on a regular basis, tip the sommelier, or wine steward (usually $1.00 per bottle), and do the same for the bartender, hairdresser or barber, and staff in the spa and fitness center—and don't forget, upon arriving and leaving the ship, to give the baggage handler at least $1.00 to $2.00 per bag.

TIP   Because it is improper to tip the captain and officers, we recommend writing a thank-you note, telling them what you liked in particular about their ship. Be extra nice and mention any outstanding staff members by name.

6

GOOD DEALS ON A GOOD NIGHT'S SLEEP

Hotel: A refuge from home life.

— *George Bernard Shaw*

MOST TRAVELERS would probably agree with this definition, as long as they can find the right ones at the right price—something that's not always easy to do. An inside look at the hospitality industry will help you see things the same way as old George.

Obviously hotels and resorts in prime areas charge the highest rates, and their facilities—swimming pools, spas, fitness clubs, marinas, and the like—raise the price per room. Exceptions to this rule of thumb are hotels with successful casinos on the premises. Their gaming take helps pay the mortgage and salaries, so rates are often somewhat lower. Regardless of whether or not hotels or motels have casinos, or where they're located or how gorgeous or shabby they are, every single one of them has something in common: perishability. This means that any night a room is empty, the revenue is lost and gone forever. This factor accounts for why lodgings of all types turn themselves inside out not to have vacant rooms, and knowing this can make you a shrewder, more confident consumer and negotiator.

GETTING THE BEST RATES

Here's the inside scoop on getting the best rates at hotels, motels, and resorts.

- *Never accept the first rate offered.* Always ask about specials. Do it with a smile and when the front-desk person is not busy with another guest.
- *Don't drag huge pieces of heavy luggage into the lobby* and then try to bargain. A smart hotel clerk knows you're a prisoner of your bags and that it's highly unlikely you will go elsewhere, regardless of the room rates.
- *Call early.* As your arrival date nears, the demand for that room typically increases, and any discounted rate is closed out, leaving only the rack rate (hotel jargon for full rate). It always pays to book your room well in advance.
- *Call direct.* If you call the 800 toll-free chain reservation number, you will be quoted only rates authorized by the chain. The operator simply reads them off a screen and has no authority to negotiate and may not even know about special discounts. So call the hotel directly and deal directly with the manager. *Note:* At times the 800-number operator may tell you the hotel has no vacancies when in reality it may not be full at all. This is because many of the huge chains allot a limited number of rooms to the central reservation system. If you're told there's no room at the inn, call the inn directly.
- *Avoid rate add-ons.* Special requests, such as a pool or beach view, are usually more expensive than an ordinary room. If a special view doesn't matter to you, ask for the lowest rate possible.
- *Confirm.* Always get a reservation number and/or the name of the person who took your reservation. This information can be very useful should there be an error or if, when you arrive, you're told the hotel is sold out.
- *Super-saver rates.* Hotels often have what are known as "fall-back rates," which they will quote if they sense you're resisting the regular rate. They don't want you to "walk." Ask for super-saver rates, specials, discounts, convention deals, or weekend rates.

- *The AAA rate.* Many hotels and motels give at least 10-percent discounts to members of the American Automobile Association and other travel clubs. It's best to arrange this when booking.
- *Senior rate.* If you're fifty or over, ask if a senior discount is available. It varies with each hotel or motel but is often worth 10 to 15 percent off the rack rate.
- *Hotel membership rate.* Special rates are often available to members of the hotel's club. You may have to join before your arrival date. These are frequently the best discounted rates a hotel provides.
- *Government discounts.* If you're in the military or if you work for a government agency or as a government contractor, you possibly can get up to 50 percent off.
- *Corporate rates.* Business travelers should always ask for the corporate rate. Be prepared to show your business card or letterhead.
- *Frequent flyer.* Many hotels and motels have teamed up with airlines to provide discounts for frequent-flyer members. If you are a frequent-flyer member, mention it when booking.
- *Convention rates.* When large sporting groups or convention-eers come to a city, the local convention and visitor's bureau usually organizes discounts at the major hotels. Always tell the reservationist if you are attending a function in order to qualify for the reduced rate.
- *Shareholder rate.* If you are a stockholder in a publicly held company in the travel business, such as Marriott or Disney, ask for a discount.
- *Package rates.* Packages are used to boost overall revenue. They range from an overnight room with breakfast to deluxe golf, tennis, scuba diving, and family packages. They tend to be offered seasonally or on the weekends.
- *Long-term-stay rates.* If you are planning an extended vacation or are relocating to a new area, ask for a long-term stay rate. These typically require a stay of at least five to seven consecutive nights.
- *Good Samaritan rates.* Many independent hotel operators and some major chains give special rates for those who are experiencing hardship—such as visiting a family member in a

hospital or going to a funeral—as well as for storm or fire victims or for persons who are stranded on the road.

- *Travel agent or travel industry.* If you or an immediate member of your family is a travel agent or works in the travel industry, you may get a reduced rate.

Sold Out? Maybe, but Probably Not

Here are some other points to keep in mind. Virtually every hotel has restricted periods. Business hotels, for example, are filled during the week but look for tourists on the weekends; just the opposite tends to be true for resort hotels. Also, check at the last minute for accommodations that were previously "sold out." The convention may have been canceled or the expected crowd didn't show up or maybe the home team didn't make it to the finals. Many "sold out" hotels actually have space available in a "suite connector," which is the living-room portion of the suite. If you're willing to sleep on a sofa bed, ask if you can rent the connector portion of a suite that's rented to someone else. Ask if there are any "out of service" rooms—the problem may only be a faulty TV set.

Travel Trivia

Men Vs. Women: According to a survey done by the Novotel New York, a hotel at Broadway and West Fifty-second Street in Manhattan, men and women are indeed different:

- Of the people who locked themselves out of their rooms: 70 percent were women; 30 percent were men.
- Of the 30 percent who were in various stages of undress in the corridor: 65 percent were women; 35 percent were men.
- Men average two towels per day; women, four towels.
- Items men leave behind: aftershave and shoes
- Items women leave behind: nightgowns
- Who leaves a cleaner room? Men.

Hotel-ese

- *Deluxe* hotels have personalized, European-style service; fewer than 350 rooms.
- *Luxury hotels* have mostly executive clientele; 400 or more rooms.
- *First-class* hotels have primarily business and private clientele; up to 1,200 rooms.
- *Convention* hotels have large meeting spaces; 1,500 rooms or more.
- *Tourist hotels* are chain affiliated or independent economy hotels without luxury and amenities; 500 to 1,000 rooms.

(*Source: Lodging Index*)

Finally, don't forget to look into small hotels. They may be more or less expensive but because they are less well known and not always a part of a chain, they are less apt to be sold out. They also tend to be more personal, often more charming and intimate than the huge business hotels. *The Small Hotel Directory* lists one hundred carefully selected hotels in the medium and expensive price range in the United States and abroad. To obtain a copy ($9.95), call (800) 327–3633.

WHERE TO FIND HOTEL DISCOUNTS

As we've stated, hotels want your head on their pillows. And just as airlines sell empty seats to consolidators, hotels make deals with discounters and publishers of discount coupon books. Take advantage of them.

Hotel-Discount Companies

The following hotel-discount companies (also known as consolidators) give anywhere from 20 to 70 percent off rack or corporate rates. Always ask what the cancellation policy is prior to booking rooms through a consolidator.

$ TIP After getting a rate on a given hotel, call that hotel directly and see if an even lower price is available.

- Capital Reservation, in Washington, D.C. (800-847-4832), knows the area's hotels extremely well.
- Express Reservations, in Boulder, Colorado (800-356-1123), books forty hotels in New York and Los Angeles.
- Hotel Reservations Network, in Dallas, Texas (800-964-6835), books hotels in more than twenty U.S. cities and in London and Paris. Can help you get rooms during "sold-out" periods, although not at a discount.
- Quikbook, in New York City (800-789-9887), books hotels in ten U.S. cities. Tries hard to please callers.
- Room Exchange, in New York City (800-846-7000), books some 22,000 hotels in the United States, Mexico, Bermuda, and the Caribbean.

Half-Price Hotels Abroad

The dollar doesn't always buy as nice a hotel room in foreign countries as it does here at home. One way to keep the cost down when sleeping abroad is to use a half-price hotel room program. You can do this by purchasing a directory of participating hotels or by joining a club that then issues a directory to members. The major ones have more than 2,000 hotels. In order to get the discount, you call or fax the hotel directly, usually about thirty days in advance, and give them your membership number. If the hotel is not too full at the time you plan to arrive, you'll get a discount. (Don't ask your travel agent to arrange this type of discount as half-price hotels are not commissionable.)

CAUTION Not all discounts are really 50 percent off. Sometimes you get 20 to 40 percent off, occasionally only 5 to 10 percent off. A small discount, however, is better than no discount at all.

Some discount programs are better suited to certain geographical areas than others. (Check the table on page 113.) Call and ask about the geographical areas you're likely to visit before signing up with any program.

SLEEPING CHEAPER

There are also places that offer really basic accommodations for only a few dollars a night that are not part of the organized hospitality industry. For example, an ashram run by Sydda Yoga in picturesque South Fallsburg, New York, has very low rates, but you have to get up at 4:00 a.m. to do an assigned task. Here are some other places with low rates and later wakeup times:

- *COLLEGES AND UNIVERSITIES.* Colleges and universities often rent out dormitory rooms and suites to tourists at low prices. As a bonus you get to enjoy the school's facilities—tennis courts, pool, library, gym, even an occasional lecture. Campus accommodations range in price from $15 to $30 a night. For a copy of *Budget Lodging Guide,* specializing in campus lodging, send $14.95 plus $2.00 shipping to Campus Travel Service, Box 5468, Fullerton, CA 92838. This annual directory lists 700 U.S., Canadian, and foreign

Half-Price Discount Programs

Program/Phone	Cost	Areas
America At 50% Discount (800) 248-2783	$14.95	United States
Encore Preferred (800) 638-0930	$49.00	United States, United Kingdom, Canada
Entertainment Publications (800) 445-4137	varies	Europe, United States, Canada
Access Development (800) 331-8867	varies	Austria, Germany, France
ITC (800) 342-0558	$49.00	Asia, South Pacific
Privilege Card International (800) 236-9732	$74.95	Caribbean, Bermuda United Kingdom, Mexico

colleges and universities as well as B&Bs, YMCAs, YWCAs, foreign study programs, farms and cottages, and home-exchange programs.

For information on universities throughout the United Kingdom, contact British Universities Accommodation Consortium, Box 966-ATW, University Park, Nottingham NG7 2RD, England; 011-44-115-950-45-71.

- *HOSTELS.* The American Youth Hostels at 733 Fifteenth Street, NW, Suite 840, Washington, DC 20005 (202-783-6161), publishes a directory that's free if you're a member; otherwise, it costs $8.00. This organization publishes two other publications: *Hostelling International's Guide to Budget Accommodations,* one for Europe and the Mediterranean and one for Africa, America, Asia, and Australia, at $13.95 each. Historic Hostels, which describes architecturally interesting hostels, has a directory for $3.00.

- *BED & BREAKFAST ESTABLISHMENTS.* Bookstores and libraries are filled with B&B directories, but to get you started from home, send a SASE to Bed & Breakfast Reservation Services Worldwide, Inc., Box 14841, Baton Rouge, LA 70898; (504) 336-4035.

  If you want to book a B&B in the United Kingdom, France, or Italy, before leaving the United States, get in touch with Hometours International, P.O. Box 11503, Knoxville, TN 37939; (800) 367-4668. This agency will also book air and rail travel and car rentals. Prices, if booked in the United States, start at $26 per person and go up to $66 for the best rooms, including VAT, service, and a hearty English breakfast. Children under age eight are usually free if they stay in their parents' room.

  $ TIP If more than three people book at the same time, there's a 7-percent discount.

- *RETREATS.* If you're looking for peace and quiet, you'll find that retreat centers and guest houses are oases of calm where anyone can recharge body and soul, whether single, a couple, or a family. For example, you can stay at the California Mission San Luis Rey Retreat Center, complete with swimming pool and spa, for about $35 a night. For an average price of $30 to $40 per person per night, including three meals a day, you can stay at retreats in forty-nine states and fourteen countries. Many retreat centers simply ask for a donation or gift. They all are church- or religious-affiliated, safe, serene, and often in extraordinarily beautiful settings. You do not have to be religious, however, to stay at one. Guest houses range from elegant English manor houses to cabins in Colorado.

Check out 450 other inexpensive retreat centers in *U.S. & Worldwide Guide to Retreat Center Guest Houses* by John and Mary Jensen. Contact CTS Publications, Box 8355, Newport Beach, CA 92660, and send $15.95 (add $2.00 for first-class postage) or call (714) 720–3729. This is the only such guide we know of published in North America or Europe.

- *MONASTERIES, ABBEYS, AND CONVENTS.* Spain's General Office of Tourism, 50 Maria de Molina, 28071 Madrid, publishes a free list of seventy-five monasteries, abbeys, and convents that take guests.

- *MOTELS.* There are many cheap motels around the United States. They are often individually owned even though they have well-known franchise names such as Comfort, Holiday Inn Express, or Rodeway. When booking in person, particularly if the motel is the non-chain, mom-and-pop variety, look behind the clerk at the keys hanging on their hooks. If there are a lot of keys, there are probably a lot of unoccupied rooms, and you can get a good rate. Before you decide to stay, however, check the room: Is it clean? Does it have a phone that connects directly to the office? Is there a deadbolt lock, a peephole in the door? Are the corridors interior ones, or can they be accessed directly from the street or parking lot? The answers to these questions should determine your decision.

Sleeping Cheaper in New York City

Here are four ways to save money when staying in Manhattan:

1. Every year the New York Convention & Visitors Bureau updates its list of more than one hundred promotional hotel packages. They include Broadway shows, sightseeing excursions, shopping discounts, complimentary meals, and parking. Rates start at $65 a night. Call (212) 397-8222 for a free copy.

2. These New York hotels are clean but not fancy:
   Carlton Arms Hotel, 160 East 25th Street, (212) 679-0680
   Excelsior Hotel, 45 West 81st Street, (212) 362-9200
   Gramercy Park, 2 Lexington Avenue, (212) 475-4320
   Herald Square, 19 West 31st Street, (212) 279-4017
   Madison Towers, Madison Avenue at 38th Street, (212) 802-0600
   Milford Plaza, Eighth Avenue, theater district, (212) 869-3600
   Olcott Hotel, 27 West 72nd Street, (212) 877-4200
   Wellington Hotel, 57th Street (across from Carnegie Hall), (212) 247-3900
   Wolcott Hotel, 31st Street (west of Fifth Avenue), (212) 268-2900

3. Get a free copy of the helpful brochure *Nine to Five: The Insider's Business Guide to Getting Around, Getting Things Done in Manhattan*, which covers a myriad of things such as clean public rest rooms, small public parks, an address finder, emergency help numbers, what's open twenty-four hours a day, etc. Write to Manhattan East Suite Hotels, 500 West 37th Street, New York, NY 10018; or call (212) 465-3600.

4. Stay in a B&B in Manhattan. City Lights has rooms with bath that start around $70 per person; more glamorous digs begin at $100. Contact City Lights, Box 20355, Cherokee Station, New York, NY 10028; (212) 737-7049.

LIGHTHOUSES

If you have an urge to sleep in a lighthouse, you can. Here are nine that will welcome you. Ask if there are kitchen facilities, linens, electricity, telephones, and showers, and get the specific location. They vary from very basic with no facilities to quite luxurious— you'll want to know in advance. Some are on paved, marked roads, while others are on off-the-beaten path dirt roads.

Point Montara Lighthouse
Box 7370
Montara, CA 94037
(415) 728-7177

Pigeon Point Lighthouse
Pigeon Point Road
Pescadero, CA 94060
(415) 879-0633

Tibbetts Point Lighthouse
RR 1
Cape Vincent, NY 13618
(315) 654-3450

Point Arena Lighthouse
Box 11
Point Arena, CA 95468
(707) 882-2777

Big Bay Point Lighthouse
3 Lighthouse Road
Big Bay, MI 49808
(906) 345-9957

Rose Island Lighthouse
Box 1419
Newport, RI 02840
(401) 847-4242

Selkirk Lighthouse
Box 228
Pulaski, NY 13142
(315) 298-6688

Isle au Haut Lighthouse
Box 26
Isle au Haut, ME 04645
(207) 367-2261

East Brother Island Light Station
117 Park Place
Point Richmond, CA 94801
(510) 233-2385

HOMESTAYS

Here's an interesting and homey approach to sleeping around the world. A homestay is an all-inclusive travel program that includes round-trip airfare (usually from either U.S. coast), and lodging in someone's house, often with meals with the family or kitchen privileges or both. The typical homestay runs two weeks, living with English-speaking hosts in two or three different cities. The hosts are often selected according to your interests or occupation. They may actually be on vacation, too, so they can spend time guiding you around their locale. You generally have your own bedroom and bathroom. With some homestays, two travelers are placed in each home, although single and family placements can be arranged, too. Smoking and nonsmoking preferences are also taken into consideration.

One of our favorites is American-International Homestays, which has programs in Berlin, Budapest, Prague, Crakow, Tashkent, Riga and Vilnius, St. Petersburg, Moscow, Kiev, Bishkek, Beijing, Shanghai, Ulan Bator, and Irkutsk/Lake Baikal.

For a list of homestay organizations, see the table on page 120.

TRADING PLACES: HOME EXCHANGE

A great way to have a vacation and avoid hotel/motel costs is to trade your house or apartment for someone else's. In this way, you get to really "live in" and not just "visit" the city or country. The people you exchange with also may give you the use of their boat, country club, domestic service, and other nice things.

Begin by contacting the agents listed in the sidebar on page 121. For a membership fee in the neighborhood of $50 to $85, these agents will list your property, often accompanied by a picture. Here are some hints for first-time traders:

- Start planning about a year in advance.
- Write or talk on the phone to potential swappers in order to get to know them.

Major International Budget Hotel/Motel Chains

Budgetel Inns	(800) 4-BUDGET
Clubhouse Inns	(800) CLUB-INN
Comfort Inns	(800) 4-CHOICE
Country Inns	(800) 456-4000
Courtyard Marriott	(800) 321-2211
Days Inns	(800) 325-2525
Econo Lodge	(800) 4-CHOICE
Fairfield Inn	(800) 228-2800
Friendship Inns	(800) 4-CHOICE
Hampton Inn	(800) HAMPTON
HoJo Inn	(800) 654-2000
Holiday Inn Express	(800) HOLIDAY
La Quinta	(800) 531-5900
Motel 6	(800) 466-8356
Ramada	(800) 2-RAMADA
Red Roof Inns	(800) THE-ROOF
Super 8	(800) 800-8000
Travelodge	(800) 255-3050

- If possible, have a friend who lives nearby take a look at the house. What's described as a castle could be something slightly less. Don't trust the photo.
- Be wary of swapping with someone very young or with groups. They may not be as careful with your possessions as you would wish.
- Ask about the location. Is it near a bus stop or subway stop, or will you need a car?
- Check your homeowners insurance policy. Are you covered for any damage they might incur? For any accidents they might have while on your property? Should you get a floater? Extra liability?
- Put any valuables and priceless mementos in a locked "off-limits" room or closet or in your safe-deposit box.

- Ask about feeding pets, watering plants, and what items you can and cannot use (and vice versa).
- Agree upon cleanliness standards and who pays the utilities—you don't want a lot of long-distance calls on your phone bill.
- Get in writing that your swapper will pay the replacement value of anything damaged; always get an up-front security deposit as well.
- Use the contract available from the home-swap network.

Homestay Organizations

Name, Address, Phone	Country
American-International Homestays Box 1754 Nederland, CO 80306 (800) 876-2048	Eastern Europe, Russia, China
Elderhostel Box 1959 Wakefield, MA 01880 (617) 426-7788	Europe, Asia New Zealand, Mexico
Friendship Force, Inc. 57 Forsyth Street, NW Atlanta, GA 30303 (404) 522-9490	Europe
Servas 11 John Street New York, NY 10038 (212) 267-0252	United States and eighty other countries
Visiting Friends, Inc. Box 231 Lake Jackson, TX 77566 (409) 297-7367	United States

RENTALS

A logical alternative to trading places if you want to stay awhile is to rent. You can rent anything from a studio apartment to a country estate or a houseboat. Most agents specialize in a few countries, but the ones listed below generally cover wide geographical areas. Remember to book several months in advance. Europeans often reserve their vacation houses a full year ahead of time, and, to some extent, you are competing with them. Be careful about the nuances of language: A "ranch" may be a down-at-the-heels farm. Make certain you know if linens will be supplied and get the name of someone to contact if you need a plumber or some other repair. Be prepared to pay the full rent in advance, even if it's for a month, and possibly a refundable security deposit. Finally, find out what the firm's cancellation policy is.

If you don't want to deal with a broker, you can take a different approach and try to make arrangements on your own. Magazines and newspapers, such as the *International Herald Tribune, the New York Times,* and big-city newspapers, have classified ads. If Europe is your destination, pick up a copy of Globe Pequot's *Guide to Vacation Rentals in Europe* ($14.95; write P.O. Box 833, Old Saybrook, CT 06475 or call 800–243–0495). If you're a free spirit and don't mind waiting until you arrive in the country or city where you want to be, check local tourist offices for listings or book a hotel room for a day or two and shop around with a local real-estate agent.

For a country cottage in France, known as a *gite,* get a copy of *Gites Guide,* published annually by FHG Publications of Paisley, Scotland; $17.95 in U.S. bookstores. It lists more than 1,200 gites

---

Home-Exchange Agents

Intervac U.S.	(800) 756–HOME
Teacher Swap	(516) 244–2845
The Invented City	(800) 788–CITY
Trading Homes International	(800) 877–8723

in English, with a picture of each and directions about how to reserve them.

Note: Two travel clubs that arrange luxury rentals for members are Hideaways International in Portsmouth, New Hampshire (800-843-4433), and the Preferred Travelers Club in Lanham, Maryland (800-638-0930), which also arranges yachts, cruises, and hotels.

TIME-SHARES

If you've discovered an area you like, you may be able to buy a week or month's stay for once a year for the next ten to twenty-five years in a time-share program. These programs are available around the world for villas, resorts, and apartments. You pay a purchase price for the week or month plus an annual maintenance fee.

Before buying a time-share, check the classifieds in the local newspapers; you may be able to purchase the same or similar property in the secondary market for a lot less. Buy the best time you can afford—Christmas, Easter, presidents' birthdays—even if you have to pay a little more because it will make it easier in the future to trade or sell. Before writing out a check, talk with other time-share owners, the local chamber of commerce, and Better Business Bureau. Scam artists have found this to be fertile territory with naive, uninformed consumers.

One day your spouse or your children may ask, "Do we have to go back *there* again?" Then the bloom is off the rose and it's time to either trade your time-share or sell it.

To try a new area, contact Interval International (800-843-8843) or Resort Condominiums International (800-446-1700); for a fee these organizations will try to find someone with whom you can trade your time-share.

You can also try to sell your time-share. You may not get what you paid for it if the economy is weak or if you don't have many years left. To sell, place ads in real-estate or travel sections of newspapers, both at home and in the area where the time-share is located. The developer or manager may be willing to buy it back or to contact other time-share owners on the property.

Local real-estate brokers may want to handle it for you on a commission basis.

Whether you are purchasing, trading, or selling, always consult an experienced real-estate lawyer and proceed cautiously, bearing in mind that this is not really an investment; it's an arrangement that guarantees you a vacation spot every year for a limited time, in a given place. That's all.

Read *Consumer's Guide to Resort and Urban Timesharing*, available for $3.00 from American Resort Development Association, 1220 L Street, NW, Washington, DC 20005; (202) 371-6700.

PLAYING IT SAFE

Nothing ruins a trip faster than being robbed, but by exercising common sense you can reduce your chances of being a victim. If you insist on traveling with valuables, be aware that a hotel's liability for items you place in a room safe or the hotel's safe is really very limited. Laws vary by state, but they are essentially written to protect the innkeepers from huge liability claims. Call the hotel in advance to discuss its policy. Make sure that the policy adequately covers your items. Also check your homeowners policy regarding coverage. **BEST BET** Leave precious things at home, or in your safe-deposit box.

Anyone traveling alone, but particularly a woman, needs to take special precautions. Ask for a room that is in a well-lighted area of the corridor and, if you get in late, have the bellman accompany you to your room. When picking up or leaving your key, be extremely circumspect about revealing your room number.

Here are six safety tips:

1. *Don't flash cash, jewelry, car keys, or hotel-room keys.* Use hidden money belts rather than fanny packs for valuables. Fanny packs not only advertise just where your valuables are located, they also scream out: *Tourist!* So do guidebooks and maps.

2. *When leaving your hotel key at the front desk,* make certain that the hotel personnel puts it away at once. Better yet, unless it has a humongous attachment, keep it with you.

International Rental Agents

At Home Abroad	(212) 421-9165
Barclay International Group	(800) 466-1769
Caribbean Destinations	(800) 888-0897
Castles, Cottages, & Flats	(617) 742-6030
Chez Vous	(415) 331-2535
Europa Let	(800) 462-4486
The French Experience	(212) 986-3800
Home At First	(800) 5-CELTIC
Hometours International	(800) 367-4668
Interhome	(201) 882-6864
Landmark Trust UK	011-44-628-825-925
Rent a Home International	(800) 488-7368
Rentals in Italy	(800) 726-6702
Vacanze Italia & France	(800) 533-5405
Vacation Home Rentals Worldwide	(800) 633-3284
Villas International	(800) 221-2260

3. *When you leave your hotel room,* leave on one light and a radio or TV playing softly.
4. *Hanging out the* MAID SERVICE *sign* advertises the fact that you've left the room.
5. *Travel with a mini flashlight.*
6. *If a fire breaks out in your hotel, leave immediately* (provided the door handle is cool), taking your room key with you. If there's smoke in the hall, wet two towels and put them around your head and proceed to the fire exit. If the door handle in your room is hot, that means there's a fire in the corridor; call the front desk and let them know where you are. Hang a sheet out the window and then close the window. If smoke is coming in, close the space under the door with damp towels, cover your nose and mouth with a wet

washcloth or towel, and stay close to the floor until help arrives.

CONCIERGES: GETTING JUST WHAT YOU NEED IN ANY CITY

Travel writer C. Paul Luongo has the inside scoop on how a hotel concierge can get you what you want—and in a hurry. Luongo, who's dealt with a number of concierges over the years, has even come up with some things you probably never knew you wanted, but now you will.

Here's an alphabetical potpourri of what a concierge can arrange, obtain, or find out for you.

Appraisals—of jewelry, art work, antiques, etc.
Babysitting—for an hour or a day
Bagels—the best in town
Boats—rent everything from a canoe to a yacht
Business cards—printed in any language
Clothing—for any occasion, including costume parties, plus pressing, mending, and tailoring
Couriers—to deliver anything anywhere
Dinner parties—in the hotel, on a yacht, in a park
Discos and dancing—where to go depending upon your age and sexual inclinations
Emergency medical service—doctors, dentists, psychiatrists, podiatrists, acupuncturists, etc.
Escorts—to accompany you to parties or about town
Flowers and plants—bouquets, bushes, potted palms
Games—a tennis partner, bridge foursome, jogging pal, chess mate
Gifts—for any occasion, for anyone
Haircare—cuts, color, sets, perms, wigs
Information—on just about anything
Jacks—for an automobile, van, or truck
Jeeves—where to find your own butler
Jewelry—where to find it; how to get it appraised
Jogging—location of a safe track or route

Kennels—where to put Fido
Kosher—restaurants and food
Lessons—dancing, language, acting, etiquette, bridge
Limo service—to anywhere, if you're willing to pay
Makeup and/or massage—in your room or elsewhere
Newspapers—out-of-town, out-of-the-country
Notary service—in an instant
Off-site betting—with tips
Packages—pickup, delivery, wrapping, mailing
Pet services—sitting, walking, patting, feeding, boarding
Photographers—for passports or portrait
Quilts—and blankets and pillows (soft, hard, square, round)
Restaurants—selection and hard-to-get reservations
Religious services—time, place, and proper attire
Secretarial services—from typing to transcription
Soap—or perfume or cologne or oil—your favorite
Tickets—to the hottest shows or sports events in town or for a
plane or train—even the *QE 2*
Tours—around the city, behind the scenes, etc.
Translation—A to Z
Unisex—clothes, haircuts, etc.
U-haul—and storage sources, if you shopped until you dropped
Videos—VCR movies of your party, wedding, trip
Water fun—swimming pools and dinner cruises
Xeroxing—and printing services—twenty-four hours
Youth—playgrounds, trips, outings, activities
Zoos—from large to small

Following are five ways to ensure the best service at your hotel.

1. Stop by the concierge's desk and introduce yourself.
2. Tell him or her how long you'll be staying and what you
   might need.
3. Smile and be polite.
4. Give the concierge a little advance notice of your request.
5. *Don't forget to tip:* Although tipping is not required, you'll
   long be remembered favorably if you do; it can be anywhere
   from $5 to $20, or 8 percent to 15 percent of the cost of the

service rendered. It's also smart and nice to call or write the hotel manager, complimenting the concierge by name.

As Jim Roberts, concierge at the Jefferson Hotel in our nation's capital, said, "As long as it's legal, we will do, locate, and go anywhere, anytime, for anything. No request is too odd."

So keep that in mind the next time you check into a hotel.

Psst: Even if you're not staying at a hotel, you can use the services of the concierge, but make it clear up front that you'll tip.

Help Us Keep This Guide Up to Date

Every effort has been made by the author and editors to make this guide as accurate and useful as possible. However, many things can change after a guide is published—establishments close, phone numbers change, facilities come under new management, etc.

We would love to hear from you concerning your experiences with this guide and how you feel it could be made better and be kept up to date. While we may not be able to respond to all comments and suggestions, we'll take them to heart and we'll also make certain to share them with the author. Please send your comments and suggestions to the following address:

The Globe Pequot Press
Reader Response/Editorial Department
P.O. Box 833
Old Saybrook, CT 06475

Or you may e-mail us at:
editorial@globe-pequot.com

Thanks for your input, and happy travels!